NATIONAL EXPRESS H

Colin Lloyd
Bill Potter

Capital Transport

ISBN 185414 188 0

Third Edition

Published by Capital Transport Publishing
38 Long Elmes, Harrow Weald, Middlesex

Printed by Bath Midway Press Ltd
Midlands Industrial Estate, Holt, Wiltshire

Contents

The front cover photo of N48MDW at Milton Keynes and the back cover photo of Airlink liveried M109PWN at Heathrow Airport are by Tony Wilson.

The contents are correct to June 1996.

NATIONAL EXPRESS – The Historical Background

Although the stagecoach could undoubtedly be classed as the forerunner of the present long distance coach network, it was not until after the First World War that express coach services really came into their own.

In 1919 the Elliott brothers, whose coaches carried the 'Royal Blue' fleet name, and who had actually run one of the earlier horse drawn services, introduced a limited form of express coach service operating between Bournemouth and London. However, Greyhound Motors of Bristol are acknowledged as introducing the first daily, all year round, motorised express coach service in Britain. Their service, introduced in 1925, linked Bristol with London and expanded rapidly. Many other operators, able to see the commercial benefits of long distance travel, introduced similar services in the following years.

One of the most successful coach entrepreneurs was George Reddings. From a base in Cheltenham in 1926 he established 'Black and White Motorways', one of the great names in the history of coaching.

Until 1930 there had been no nationwide regulation of services, leaving the way open for any operator to provide whatever service he thought fit. This in turn resulted in various degrees of unacceptable competitive behaviour throughout the country, although it must be emphasised that the worst cases of 'predatory' tactics were confined to the local bus operation.

The 1930 Road Traffic Act introduced a system of licensing covering drivers, conductors and routes operated. The Act successfully brought order to the rapidly growing chaotic and somewhat haphazard industry. As each bus and coach service now required a licence, granted by the Traffic Commissioners, before operation could commence, operators found it much harder to introduce new services. The new system of licensing provided the stability for expansion. Early co-operation among the operators gave rise to the foundation of operating 'pools' offering greatly increased travel opportunities to the ever increasing number of coach passengers.

Two famous coaching 'Pools' were Associated Motorways, based at Cheltenham, and London Coastal Coaches which was centred on London Victoria. The new Victoria Coach Station was opened in London in 1932.

By the outbreak of war in 1939, a comprehensive network of express services, provided by a number of operators and pools, had been established throughout Britain. During the early years of the war services soldiered on, carrying evacuees, servicemen and ordinary passengers until all express operations were cancelled by government order in November 1942. After the war ended, services were re-established quickly and by the summer of 1946 a start had been made re-forming the networks. Such was the demand for travel in the immediate post-war years that passenger growth continued through until the late 1950s, when traffic peaked.

From then on, the number of private cars began to increase with a matched decline in coach traffic. In 1959 the opening of the first stretch of Motorway (now the M6) around Preston and the M1 brought new opportunities for express services for companies such as Standerwick, Ribble's coaching subsidiary, and Midland Red, who specifically developed their own integral motorway coach for such operation.

In 1959 the first 'Gay Hostess' went into Ribble service from the North West to London, Scotland and the South West. These prestigious vehicles were Leyland Atlanteans fitted with air suspension and a higher rated rear axle. On these chassis were mounted Weymann bodies which incorporated refreshment servery, toilet and an additional luggage area.

By the late sixties most bus companies, with the exception of municipal and small independent operators, had formed into two main groups, the state owned Tilling Group and the BET (British Electric Traction) Group. In March 1968 both groups were brought together by the government under the state owned Transport Holding Company. Later that year the government introduced a Transport Act designed to create an integrated public passenger transport system across the country. One of the major provisions of the Act was the setting up of the National Bus Company, which was formed on 28th November 1968, operations commencing on 1st January 1969 with the acquisition of the assets and shareholding of the Transport Holding Company.

By the end of 1969 NBC had bought the BET Group as well and evolved some 44 operational units to run the 93 bus companies now under its wing. At this time the fleet strength of NBC was 21,000 and the number of staff employed was over 81,000.

From the beginning, the Directors of what was now the biggest road passenger transport operation in Europe sought to bring together the coaching activities of each constituent operator. This provided for a standard policy on express coach operation to eliminate any duplication of services inherited from previous limited competition between the separate companies. Such a change was also expected to benefit the passenger.

Following the establishment by NBC of the Central Activities Group in April 1972, the 'National' brand name was introduced and the now famous white livery began to appear on coaches as a first stage in offering a nationwide standard and a recognisable product to customers. The winter of 1973/74 saw the publication of the first comprehensive coach timetable that included details of the entire 'National' network. The new brand name of 'NATIONAL EXPRESS' first appeared on publicity in 1974, and on vehicles some four years later in 1978.

During 1978 the 'EXTRA' computer reservations system was brought into operation giving an improved service to customers and booking agents. This was followed in 1979 with a major market research programme. Every passenger on every journey was asked why, when and where they were travelling. This information subsequently became useful in winning a number of battles in the Traffic Courts around the country by proving the need for new services, additional coaches and lower fares on key inter-urban routes.

Typical of the Red & White coach fleet in the late sixties was the Bristol RELH6L with ECW bodywork. Seen in Monmouth during September 1974 is their RC569, the first of this batch to gain the then new National white livery. *Peter J. Relf*

Originally new to Ribble in 1970, National Welsh UC970 was one of a pair acquired in 1981 with the absorption of Jones of Aberbeeg. It was a Leyland Leopard PSU4A/4R with Plaxton Panorama Elite bodywork fitted with 36 reclining seats and was photographed in Reading in September 1981. *Peter J. Relf*

United Counties 214 was one of five Bristol REL6HGs new in 1973, which had bus style bodies fitted with coach seats. July 1974 finds the vehicle in Christchurch en route to Stevenage on route 766. *Peter J. Relf*

Midland Red 6452 was one of the Leyland Leopard PSU4B/4R coaches with the Plaxton Panorama Elite bodywork. London's Park Lane provides the backdrop of this shot taken in July 1981, by which time the famous National Express logos were beginning to appear on many operators' coaches.
Peter J. Relf

Right ECW's final coach design for the Bristol RE is illustrated here by National Welsh's RC2374. Originally new to Red & White in 1974 as RC474, it was a Bristol RELH6L seen here in Farnham in May 1981 homeward bound to Cardiff.
Peter J. Relf

The coming into effect of the 1980 Transport Act, on 6th October 1980, changed the basis of express coach operation overnight. The Act removed the licensing restrictions which had been in force since 1930 and introduced competition on long distance coach services. National Express and the, then, main Scottish express coach operator, Scottish Citylink Coaches, faced new competition from a host of established bus and coach operators who sought to diversify into this new area of long distance coach operation. This removed the routes monopoly given to operators through the licensing system and presented the established operator with competition.

The management of National Express was given a free hand by NBC to meet and respond to this competition, though no subsidy was forthcoming. Many of the new operations were curtailed within a few months. Similarly, a joint venture of several operators under the title 'British Coachways' failed to capture sufficient business and eventually ceased. However the actions did lead to a significant increase in passengers by some fifty per cent for National Express.

Some coach operators fared better than most, and several of these are now well established in the marketplace. Two of these, Trathens from the West Country and Cotters from Scotland, had introduced up-market coaches equipped with hostesses, refreshments and toilets. This type of service was similar to that offered by, amongst others, Standerwick prior to their becoming part of the National Bus Company. In 1981, National Express entered into an agreement with Trathens to co-operate in the running of the West Country services to this higher specification and this standard of service quality was given the name 'Rapide'. The Rapide service re-introduced a Hostess or Steward service of light refreshments to each seat with the coaches on these services having toilet/washroom facilities, air suspension and reclining seats. These on-board facilities cut out the need for intermediate stops offering some 20% reduction in journey times. The public demand for the Rapide services was very high and brought about the introduction of a new generation of double-deck coach to cater for the higher number of customers.

Initially part of the Royal Blue allocation when new in 1975, Western National 2426 was later transferred to National Express duties. As with most National Express vehicles of the period, it was the ubiquitous Leyland Leopard with Plaxton Panorama Elite III that was seen passing through Basingstoke in July 1981. *Peter J. Relf*

Hamilton's of Uxbridge acquired MDF 120P in 1985 from National Travel (West) in full National Express livery, having originated with National Travel (South West) in 1976. This Leyland Leopard PSU3C/4R, with Duple Dominant I bodywork shown on The Embankment in central London, had been modified with the later Duple Dominant IV front grille when seen in May 1986. *Peter J. Relf*

By the mid-1970s, the Duple/Plaxton duopoly was finally broken with the emergence of Willowbrook as a major supplier of coach bodies to NBC companies. This example is the Spacecar design. Although new to Shamrock & Rambler in 1977 as their 400, when seen at Chippenham in July 1983, REL400R had managed to pass through the fleets of National Travel (South West) and Hants & Dorset before returning to Shamrock & Rambler as 3020. *Peter J. Relf*

National Express became a limited company in May 1984 although still part of NBC. At this time the revenue from each service was retained by the individual operating company, with National Express marketing, planning and overhead costs being met out of this revenue. Any profit was retained by the operating bus company after staffing and other costs had been met. From April 1986, and to prepare for eventual privatisation, this policy changed with National Express paying the operating company on a contractual basis and becoming totally responsible for the revenue and the performance of the network.

On 26th October 1986 the 1985 Transport Act brought into effect deregulation of local bus services, though this had little effect on the express coach services which had become open to competition back in 1980. More important for National Express was the requirement of the Transport Act for the National Bus Company to divest itself of the operating companies.

National Holidays was the first operator to be sold, in July 1986 to Shearings, with the final operator, London Country North East, being sold in April 1988 to AJS. National Express was subject to a management buy-out on 17th March 1988.

Delivered new to Shamrock & Rambler as 3100 in 1983, BPR100Y had by June 1986, when seen at Preston Park, been owned by five different operators. It was a Leyland Tiger TRCTL11/3R with Duple Laser bodywork and at the time carried National London fleet names although owned by London Country Bus Services of Reigate. *Peter J. Relf*

The DAF-engined Bova Europa was first imported in 1981 and its light weight made it popular with operators not yet used to heavyweight products. Delivered new in 1983, this example is seen on The Embankment, London, in June 1986 whilst in the employ of Atlas Coaches of Harlesden. *Peter J. Relf*

The forerunner of the briefly successful Dennis Javelin, now gaining much favour with National Express operators, was the Dennis Falcon V. All were fitted with the Duple Goldliner IV style of bodywork. AOD647Y was new to Western National in 1982 but had gained additional Trathens fleet names when pictured at the Hogs Back, Guildford in May 1983. *Peter J. Relf*

Between 1988 and 1991, National Express Holdings Ltd, the name of the company set up to buy National Express from the National Bus Company, acquired the established North Wales bus operator, Crosville Wales; the Merseyside operator, Amberline, the ATL Holdings Group (which included Carlton PSV, the coach dealership, and the Yelloway Trathens operation) and the express services of Stagecoach Holdings Ltd based at Perth.

The acquisition of the express coach services of the Stagecoach Holdings Group on 31st July 1989 came at the same time as the long standing agreement with Scottish Citylink coaches on joint operation across the English/Scottish border came to an end. A subsidiary company, Caledonian Express, was set up to market the new Scottish network from a Head Office at the old Stagecoach premises in Perth. Tied in to the main National Express network, Caledonian Express began to grow almost immediately, particularly in competition with Scottish Citylink, at this time still part of the Scottish Bus Group. New Neoplan double-deck coaches entered service on the prestige Rapide services linking London with Scotland and new marketing initiatives were introduced matching those in England and Wales.

On 23rd July 1991, National Express Holdings Ltd was bought out by a consortium made up of a number of City investment companies and the Drawlane Transport Group. The then chairman of the Drawlane Transport Group moved from that position and became chairman of the new company, the National Express Group Ltd. The syndicate of investors, which contained some notable City Institutions, is led by ECI. Other partners include Hendersons Ventures, County NatWest, Eagle Star and Bank of Boston. Instrumental in forming the syndicate was the Drawlane Transport Group, which also provided equity and Directors for the new Holding Company, called National Express Group Ltd.

MCW of Birmingham built about 130 Metroliner double deck coaches, the majority of which went to NBC companies. Western National were one of the first to operate these high specification vehicles, with 1406 seen at St Austell in August 1985 carrying Royal Blue fleet names. *Peter J. Relf*

Although the majority of Neoplans imported into Britain were integrals, a small number were fitted with the Plaxton Paramount 4000 bodywork. West Yorkshire 2002, with the later Paramount 4000 II body style, was photographed at Golders Green carrying Northern Rose fleet names during September 1988. *Peter J. Relf*

Throughout its long and varied history, National Express has faced many changes. On 1st December 1992 the company was floated on the London Stock Exchange at a share price of 165p. The prospectus for the flotation made it clear that the group would re-focus on core activities. On 23rd March 1993 Carlton PSV Ltd was sold, leaving as the main subsidiaries National Express Ltd, Eurolines (UK) Ltd and Speedlink Airport Services Ltd. The Eurolines operation was strengthened on 5th July 1993 with the acquisition of Eurolines Nederland BV, based in Amsterdam.

Further expansion took place on 6th August 1993 when East Midlands International Airport plc was added to the group, followed in April 1995 by Bournemouth International Airport. More recently, the group merged with West Midlands Travel, the Birmingham-based bus operating group, though this is operated separately.

In March 1996 National Express acquired the Flightlink operation from Flights Travel Group, the Birmingham-based service linking West Midlands, Manchester, Heathrow and Gatwick airports. The vehicles used on this service will continue to be operated by Flights Coach Travel, a separate division within Flights Travel Group, and the beige, red and black livery will continue to be used.

To further the expansion into other areas of public transport the National Express Group tendered to the British Railways Board for several rail franchises. So far two have been awarded to the Group, the Gatwick Express service on 3rd April 1996, followed a few weeks later by the Midland Main Line franchise.

For its coach services National Express hires in by contract all of the 500 coaches required to operate its daily services, though the figure can reach around 1000 on Saturdays and bank holiday weekends. Each coach operator providing coaches has to adhere to strictly controlled specifications. Failure to do so results in financial penalties with the ultimate possibility of the loss of a contract. In this way, National Express is able to keep a check on the standard of the coaches, staff, reliability and, most importantly for National Express, the level of service and safety offered to passengers. Following extensive on-board research, a nationwide No Smoking policy was introduced aboard all coaches from 1st November 1992.

A new design of coach, the National Expressliner, was introduced in March 1989 in a joint venture between Volvo, Plaxton and National Express. The Expressliner was designed to be the standard express coach for the network to be available to all operating companies. It is fitted to Rapide specification and includes many features aimed at improving passenger comfort, convenience and safety. Fitted with 46 reclining seats, each with a tray and magazine rack, they are trimmed with grey moquette featuring the familiar National Express double N symbol in red and blue. Airline style overhead luggage lockers are fitted and to the rear are a refreshment servery, a working area for the hostess or steward and a toilet with wash basin. The conventional configuration, ie not to Rapide specification, should seat 49.

Later specifications for the Expressliner include a non-Rapide form, though the only difference is the replacement of the servery by three extra seats. At present the coaches are available only to National Express operators through leasing arrangements, though following some controversy a few were sold direct at the end of 1990.

In 1992 agreement was reached on a second generation of Expressliner, with the new model being unveiled on 23rd July. Again based on the Volvo B10M chassis it carries the latest Plaxton Première 350 design modified to the requirements of National Express which include the solid, white, rear and double N motif. The first three entered service with Amberline in early August 1992. All were initially built using the latest version of the B10M coach chassis, which features an uprated 285bhp low pollution engine. Three gearbox options are offered, two from ZF plus Volvo's own G7 unit. While the first generation of Expressliners were only available on five-year operating lease/contract maintenance agreements, the MkIIs can be purchased outright, or taken on finance and operating leases. During 1995 the options for coachwork were extended to include the Van Hool and Jonckheere products, which chassis variants include Dennis Javelins on which the Expressliner II is also available from Plaxton.

In 1996, the longest route operated on the network is the 806 service from Edinburgh to Penzance, a distance of 678 miles, while the shortest is the nine-mile route between Bristol Airport and the city centre. There are some 200 services operated on the summer timetable and the various services are listed under the heading of each contract operator. Some services are jointly operated.

National Express operates coach stations at Birmingham, Bournemouth, Leeds, Liverpool and Manchester. Victoria Coach Station in London, extensively refurbished in 1992, is operated by London Regional Transport with National Express paying a departure fee per coach. There are around 160,000 departures from VCS each year of which about 10,000 are to destinations on the European mainland.

The Digbeth Coach Station at Birmingham is the hub of the coach network, offering interchange facilities to and from all parts of the UK. Around 200 coaches pass through the station every day, carrying around 10,000 passengers.

The central bus station at Heathrow commenced re-development in January 1996. This site is gaining traffic and new Airport services have been introduced with a special AirLink livery.

National Express is the brand leader in express coach travel and now serves some 1200 destinations. During the summer months around 900 coaches operate daily through some sixty operators.

We are grateful to National Express, the operating companies, Joe Cahill, Andy Chown, David Donati, Keith Grimes, Jef Johnson, Mike Lambden, Stuart Render, Steve Sanderson and the PSV Circle for their assistance in the compilation of this book.

Although this book has been produced with the co-operation of National Express, it is not an official National Express fleet list and the vehicles are subject to variation. A few vehicles listed as being in National Express livery are no longer in regular use on National Express services as they are in excess of the age limit of seven years. The services operated by the companies are subject to variation at any time although accurate at the time of going to print. The contents are correct to June 1996.

The latest addition to the Shaw Hadwin fleet is represented by N160GRN, a Plaxton Première 350 bodied Volvo B10M-62. Victoria in May 1996 sees the coach having recently arrived on the 08.30 departure from Eastbourne of route 066. *Colin Lloyd*

Left Starting its life with Wallace Arnold in 1992, Premier 443 was one of a batch of six Plaxton Première 350s purchased in 1994 and repainted into standard National Express livery as seen here in Chesterfield in September 1995. *Tony Wilson*

Above United Counties, part of the mighty Stagecoach empire, operate route 055 between London and Rugby. Although it will no doubt stop in dense traffic in Finchley Road, 93 is seen leaving Golders Green, its last scheduled stop before arriving at Victoria. *Capital Transport*

Above Bebbs M37KAX awaits service in Buckingham Palace Road in April 1996 showing the rear end styling on the Plaxton Expressliner. *Colin Lloyd*

Right A rear nearside view at Newcastle of Northumbria 137, an integral bodied Bova FHD 12.340. The entire National Express network operated by Northumbria is made up of Bova machines. albeit with two underframe variants. *Capital Transport*

Above Yellow Buses of Bournemouth, also trading as Dorset Travel, operate a pair of these MAN coaches with the attractive Berkhof Excellence 2000HL body. June 1995 finds their 331 at Bristol on route 333 bound for its home town. *Richard Eversden*

Right The Scania K113CRB chassis combined with the Van Hool Alizée HE body remains a rarity on National Express work, although popular with Durham Travel. May 1995 finds number 3 turning into Drummond Gate, Pimlico, having covered the 07.05 departure from Portsmouth on route 065. *Colin Lloyd*

Galloway J811 KHD is a Van Hool Alizée mounted on a DAF SB3000, not one of the most common chassis types currently in use, seen passing the Houses of Parliament on the 11.30 departure from London bound for Ipswich on route 081. This coach is now re-registered 5516PP. *Colin Lloyd*

Birmingham Coach Company operate an express service between London and Birmingham. This Scania K113CRB with Van Hool Alizée HE body is one of three vehicles to carry this non-standard livery and London Express branding. It is seen leaving Victoria in April 1996. *Colin Lloyd*

Left One of only two contractors who have so far opted for the Volvo B12 are Trathens of Plymouth. N754CYA features the Van Hool Astrobel body and was pictured at Heathrow Central Coach Station in February 1996.
Colin Lloyd

Right One of only four double deck examples left in their National Express fleet, Durham Travel 5 is an Auwaerter Neoplan with the Skyliner body. With routes 526 and 545 currently specifying double deck operation, it will be interesting to see what vehicles will be used when these Neoplans are due for replacement.
Capital Transport

Above Marketed as the Futura Club, only three low floor versions of this Bova style operate on National Express work, all with Wilts & Dorset. Number 3213 is seen leaving Victoria bound for Yeovil on route 005 in March 1996. *Colin Lloyd*

Right Northumbria 134 is a Bova FHD12.290 with the integral Futura body and is one of five with this type of underframe operated by Northumbria. It was seen passing through Northampton in April 1996. *Tony Wilson*

Above Bluebird buses operate route 593 between London and Perth. Their 623 is one of only a handful of Volvo B10M-61s in service, the 60 and 62 variants being a more popular choice. *Colin Lloyd*

Right Starting to gain favour with a number of operators recently is the Guildford built Dennis Javelin. Selwyns 61 is seen in Edinburgh while on layover from its trip north from Warrington in August 1995. *Tony Wilson*

Above This rear offside view of Park's M628FNS at Sheffield in May 1996 shows the styling afforded to the Jonckheere Deauville 45 body. As with the Plaxton Expressliner, the absence of a rear window indicates provision for a servery. *Capital Transport*

Right Relatively few National Express operators have opted to buy Jonckheere Deauville bodies. Park's of Hamilton have, as shown by their M629FNS mounted on a Volvo B10M passing through a picturesque Edinburgh in August 1995. *Tony Wilson*

Fast approaching its seven year expiry date and consequent withdrawal from National Express duties is Ambassador 111, a Leyland Tiger with Plaxton Paramount 3500 III body seen in Stratford, London in May 1995. *Colin Lloyd*

The only examples of the Kassbohrer Setra within the National Express empire are operated by Chenery of Dickleburgh. Arriving at Victoria in August 1995 from Norwich on route 599, RYG 684 is one of five Setra coaches currently in use by Chenery. *Colin Lloyd*

Above The eastern extremity of route 007 finds Stagecoach South 8910 in Dover. This coach is one of four examples still on National Express work that was inherited with the East Kent takeover during 1993. *Paul Gainsbury*

Right Another National Express operator to deviate from standard livery is Express Travel of Speke, who introduced three Express Shuttle services based on Manchester in May 1994. Express Shuttles have since been introduced from London to Cambridge and Brighton. K504WNR, a Volvo B10M with Plaxton Expressliner II body, is seen at Liverpool in March 1996. *Tony Wilson*

Above A typical view of an interior of a National Express coach, although in this case it is one of the dedicated Air Link coaches. Note the rear servery, toilet area and seat belts. *Capital Transport*

Right Armstrong Galley is the coaching arm of Busways of Newcastle-upon-Tyne. Their National Express Air Link service is operated with an exclusive fleet of Plaxton bodied Volvo B10Ms, as typified here by 81 at Hatton Cross. *Tony Wilson*

Yorkshire Buses operate route 240 between Gatwick and Bradford using five Van Hool bodied Scania K113CRBs with dedicated Air Link livery. Their 53 is seen at Sheffield Bus Station in August 1995 en route via Wakefield. *Tony Wilson*

Still a scarcity with contractors on the National Express network is the Plaxton Excalibur. September 1995 finds Armstrong Galley 86 at Heathrow Central Coach Station on route 230 to Gatwick Airport. *Ivor Norman*

One of the few companies allowed to operate coaches in other than National Express livery is Don Smith Coaches. Maundy Thursday in April 1996 finds HIL5835 a long way from its usual route 662 covering a relief working to London. Bank Holidays usually see many strange workings to cover the extra journeys laid on. *Colin Lloyd*

Another of the operators to have received dispensation to operate a National Express service with their own livery is Chalfont Coaches of Southall. Unusually covering route 201, M861TYC is a Van Hool Alizée bodied Volvo B10M, and was found on layover in Cardiff Bus Station during September 1995. *Richard Eversden*

Yorkshire Traction is the only National Express operator to operate the Scania K93. Depicted here is number 2, formerly registered K802FWE, a Plaxton Paramount 3500 III on route 560 cruising down Park Lane in central London during March 1996. *Colin Lloyd*

Only a handful of Duple 425 integrals are used by National Express contractors, with Moore of Congleton operating a pair. This handsome machine turns into Eccleston Street at the end of its trip, still looking immaculate. *Colin Lloyd*

Acquired new in 1990, 2230 was a former Premier example which joined the North Devon fleet during 1993. One of the elder statesman of the National Express fleet, its registration was first carried by a 1961 Leyland Atlantean, new to Devon General. It is seen at Westward Ho! in September 1995. *Kevin Lane*

In 1993, the Rider Group acquired a Plaxton Première 350. Obviously pleased with their new coach, an additional trio were added to the fleet although they were Volvo B10M-62s as opposed to the B10M-60. Here 1423 arrives in Sheffield on a grey September day in 1995. *Tony Wilson*

Route 331 is unique within the National Express network in that it is the only scheduled route to be allocated a minicoach. Wessex 145, a Peugeot-Talbot Pullman, is the allocated vehicle although an Iveco Daily is also available when required. Fully repainted into Air Link livery, the coach is seen at Bristol Airport in April 1996. *Alex Mackin*

AJC COACHES

AJC Fallas of Leeds Ltd, 245 Elland Road, Leeds, LS11 8TU

650 Alton Towers– Bradford
657 Leeds–Pwllheli
561 London–Bradford
561 London–Knaresborough
664 Skegness–York

61	H114UYG	Volvo B10M-60	Plaxton Expressliner	C46FT	1991		Rapide
62	H741WWU	Volvo B10M-60	Plaxton Expressliner	C46FT	1991		Rapide
72	K524RJX	DAF SB3000DKVF601	Van Hool Alizée	C51FT	1993	Ex Hallmark, Luton, 1995	Rapide
73	K526RJX	DAF SB3000DKVF601	Van Hool Alizée	C51FT	1993	Ex Hallmark, Luton, 1995	Rapide
74	K531RJX	DAF SB3000DKVF601	Van Hool Alizée	C51FT	1993	Ex Fishwick, Leyland, 1994	Rapide
	H346JFX	Volvo B10M-60	Plaxton Expressliner	C46FT	1990	Ex Dorset Travel, 1995	Rapide
	H347JFX	Volvo B10M-60	Plaxton Expressliner	C46FT	1990	Ex Dorset Travel, 1995	Rapide

AMBASSADOR TRAVEL

Ambassador Travel (Anglia) Ltd, James Watt Close, Gapton Hall Industrial Estate, Great Yarmouth, Norfolk, NR31 0NX

081 London–Great Yarmouth
308 Aberdare–Great Yarmouth
495 London–Cromer
496 London–Cromer
497 London–Lowestoft
597 London–Great Yarmouth

100	F100BPW	Volvo B10M-61	Plaxton Expressliner	C46FT	1989	Rapide
101	F101BPW	Volvo B10M-61	Plaxton Expressliner	C46FT	1989	Rapide
106	F106CCL	Volvo B10M-61	Plaxton Expressliner	C48FT	1989	National Express
107	G107HNG	Volvo B10M-61	Plaxton Paramount 3500 III	C48FT	1989	National Express
108	G108HNG	Volvo B10M-61	Plaxton Paramount 3500 III	C46F	1989	National Express
109	G109HNG	Leyland Tiger TRCL10/3ARM	Plaxton Paramount 3500 III	C48FT	1990	National Express
111	G111HNG	Leyland Tiger TRCL10/3ARM	Plaxton Paramount 3500 III	C48FT	1990	National Express
112	G512MNG	Volvo B10M-60	Plaxton Paramount 3500 III	C46F	1990	National Express
113	G609MVG	Volvo B10M-60	Plaxton Paramount 3500 III	C46FT	1990	Rapide
121	H381TNG	Leyland Tiger TRCL10/3ARZM	Plaxton Paramount 3500 III	C48FT	1991	National Express

ARMSTRONG GALLEY

Busways Travel Services Ltd, 120 Northumberland Street, Newcastle-upon-Tyne, NE1 7DG

230 Gatwick–Newcastle
230 Gatwick–Nottingham

81	L81YBB	Volvo B10M-62	Plaxton Expressliner II	C44FT	1993		AirLink
82	L82YBB	Volvo B10M-62	Plaxton Expressliner II	C46FT	1993		AirLink
83	L83YBB	Volvo B10M-62	Plaxton Expressliner II	C46FT	1993		AirLink
84	L84YBB	Volvo B10M-62	Plaxton Expressliner II	C46FT	1993		AirLink
85	KSU462	Volvo B10M-60	Plaxton Excalibur	C46FT	1992	Ex Park's, 1993	AirLink
86	KSU463	Volvo B10M-60	Plaxton Excalibur	C46FT	1992	Ex Park's, 1993	AirLink
87	KSU464	Volvo B10M-60	Plaxton Excalibur	C46FT	1992	Ex Park's, 1993	AirLink
88	M808JTY	Volvo B10M-62	Plaxton Expressliner II	C44FT	1995		AirLink

Previous Registrations

| KSU462 | J420HDS | | KSU463 | J422HDS | | KSU464 | J424HDS | |

BADGERLINE

Bristol Omnibus Company Ltd, Enterprise House, Easton Road, Bristol, BS5 0DZ

402 London–Street
403 London–Bath
403 London–Weston-super-Mare

290	M290FAE	Dennis Javelin GX 12SDA2153	Plaxton Expressliner II	C49FT	1995	National Express
291	M291FAE	Dennis Javelin GX 12SDA2153	Plaxton Expressliner II	C49FT	1995	National Express
292	M292FAE	Dennis Javelin GX 12SDA2153	Plaxton Expressliner II	C49FT	1995	National Express
293	M293FAE	Dennis Javelin GX 12SDA2153	Plaxton Expressliner II	C49FT	1995	National Express
294	M294FAE	Dennis Javelin GX 12SDA2153	Plaxton Expressliner II	C49FT	1995	National Express
295	M295FAE	Dennis Javelin GX 12SDA2153	Plaxton Expressliner II	C49FT	1995	National Express
296	M296FAE	Dennis Javelin GX 12SDA2153	Plaxton Expressliner II	C49FT	1995	National Express

BEBBS

Bebb Travel plc, The Coach Station, Llantwit Fardre, Pontypridd, Mid Glamorgan, CF38 2HB

201 Gatwick–Swansea
320 Birmingham–Bradford
509 London–Aberdare
545 London–Pwllheli
301 Bristol–Cardiff
320 Bradford–Cardiff
509 London–Cardiff
550 London–Liverpool
310 Birmingham–Bradford
320 Brecon–Skipton
545 London–Birmingham
749 Aberdeen–Cardiff

M23JDW	Volvo B10M-62	Plaxton Première 350	C49FT	1994	National Express
M24JDW	Volvo B10M-62	Plaxton Première 350	C49FT	1994	National Express
M32KAX	Volvo B10M-62	Plaxton Expressliner II	C49FT	1995	National Express
M34KAX	Volvo B10M-62	Plaxton Expressliner II	C49FT	1995	National Express
M35KAX	Volvo B10M-62	Plaxton Expressliner II	C49FT	1995	National Express
M36KAX	Volvo B10M-62	Plaxton Première 350	C46FT	1995	National Express
M37KAX	Volvo B10M-62	Plaxton Première 350	C46FT	1995	National Express
M38KAX	Volvo B10M-62	Plaxton Première 350	C46FT	1995	AirLink
M39KAX	Volvo B10M-62	Plaxton Première 350	C46FT	1995	Rapide
M41KAX	Volvo B10M-62	Plaxton Première 350	C46FT	1995	Rapide
M42KAX	Volvo B10M-62	Plaxton Première 350	C46FT	1995	Rapide
M43KAX	Volvo B10M-62	Plaxton Première 350	C46FT	1995	Rapide
M45KAX	Volvo B10M-62	Plaxton Première 350	C46FT	1995	Rapide
N46MDW	Volvo B10M-62	Plaxton Première 350	C46FT	1995	Rapide
N47MDW	Volvo B10M-62	Plaxton Première 350	C46FT	1995	Rapide
N48MDW	Volvo B10M-62	Plaxton Première 350	C46FT	1995	National Express
N49MDW	Volvo B10M-62	Plaxton Première 350	C46FT	1995	Rapide
N51MDW	Volvo B10M-62	Plaxton Première 350	C46FT	1995	Rapide
N52MDW	Volvo B10M-62	Plaxton Expressliner II	C49FT	1995	National Express
N53MDW	Volvo B10M-62	Plaxton Expressliner II	C49FT	1995	National Express

BIRMINGHAM COACH COMPANY

Birmingham Coach Company Ltd, Cross Quays Business Park, Hallbridge Way, Tipton Road, Tividale, Warley, West Midlands, B69 3HY

225 Gatwick–Birmingham	225 Gatwick–Wolverhampton	520 London–Wolverhampton
225 Gatwick–Manchester	387 Blackpool–Coventry	545 London–Holyhead

H10	H10WLE	Scania K113TRB	Van Hool Astrobel	CH57/14CT	1990	Ex Busways, 1994	Rapide
237	M237SOJ	Scania K113CRB	Van Hool Alizée H	C44FT	1995		London Express
556	H556WTS	Volvo B10M-60	Plaxton Expressliner	C46FT	1990	Ex National Express, 1996	Rapide
657	K657BOH	Volvo B10M-60	Plaxton Expressliner II	C46FT	1993	Ex West Midlands Travel, 1996	Rapide
658	K658BOH	Volvo B10M-60	Plaxton Expressliner II	C46FT	1993	Ex West Midlands Travel, 1996	Rapide
659	K659BOH	Volvo B10M-60	Plaxton Expressliner II	C46FT	1993	Ex West Midlands Travel, 1996	Rapide
660	K660BOH	Volvo B10M-60	Plaxton Expressliner II	C46FT	1993	Ex West Midlands Travel, 1996	Rapide
682	H682FCU	Scania K113TRB	Van Hool Astrobel	CH53/14CT	1990	Ex Busways, 1994	Rapide
683	N683AHL	Scania K113CRB	Van Hool Alizée HE	C44FT	1995		Rapide
684	N684AHL	Scania K113CRB	Van Hool Alizée HE	C44FT	1995		Rapide
784	M784SOF	Scania K113CRB	Van Hool Alizée HE	C44FT	1995		London Express
785	M785SOF	Scania K113CRB	Van Hool Alizée HE	C44FT	1995		London Express

Previous Registrations;

K657BOH	K5CEN	K659BOH	K3CEN	H682FCU	H133ACU, KSU463
K658BOH	K4CEN	K660BOH	K2CEN	H10WLE	H134ACU, KSU464, H681FCU

BLUEBIRD BUSES

Bluebird Buses Ltd, Guild Street, Aberdeen AB9 2DR

593 London–Glasgow	593 London–Perth	596 London–Glenrothes	752 Kettering–Dundee

618	N618USS	Volvo B10M-62	Plaxton Expressliner II	C44FT	1995		Rapide
619	N619USS	Volvo B10M-62	Plaxton Expressliner II	C44FT	1995		Rapide
620	N620USS	Volvo B10M-62	Plaxton Expressliner II	C44FT	1995		Rapide
621	J917LEM	Volvo B10M-61	Plaxton Expressliner	C46FT	1991	Ex Express Travel, 1994	Rapide
622	J919LEM	Volvo B10M-61	Plaxton Expressliner	C46FT	1991	Ex Express Travel, 1994	Rapide
623	J455FSR	Volvo B10M-61	Plaxton Expressliner	C46FT	1992	Ex Express Travel, 1994	Rapide
624	J456FSR	Volvo B10M-61	Plaxton Expressliner	C46FT	1992	Ex Express Travel, 1994	Rapide

CHALFONT COACHES

Chalfont Coaches of Harrow Ltd, 200 Featherstone Road, Southall, Middlesex, UB2 5AQ

605 Calcot–Birmingham (NEC)   610 London–Birmingham (NEC)   685 London–Minehead   694 Luton–Birmingham (NEC)

E329FLD	Volvo B10M-61	Plaxton Paramount 3200 III	C57F	1987		White & purple
F306RMH	Volvo B10M-61	Plaxton Paramount 3500 III	C57F	1988		White & purple
H158DJU	Volvo B10M-60	Plaxton Paramount 3200 III	C57F	1990		White & purple
H487FGL	Volvo B10M-60	Van Hool Alizée	C49FT	1990	Ex Ford, Gunnislake, 1993	White & purple
M860TYC	Volvo B10M-62	Van Hool Alizée	C46FT	1994		White & purple
M861TYC	Volvo B10M-62	Van Hool Alizée	C53F	1994		White & purple
M862TYC	Volvo B10M-62	Van Hool Alizée	C53F	1995		White & purple
N197DYB	Volvo B10M-62	Van Hool Alizée	C57FT	1996		White & purple
N198DYB	Volvo B10M-62	Van Hool Alizée	C53FT	1996		White & purple

CHELTENHAM DISTRICT

Cheltenham District Traction Company Ltd, 3/4 Bath Street, Cheltenham, Gloucestershire, GL50 1YE

412 London–Gloucester

534	G534LWU	Volvo B10M-60	Plaxton Paramount 3500 III	C48FT	1990	Ex Wallace Arnold, 1993	National Express
546	G546LWU	Volvo B10M-60	Plaxton Paramount 3500 III	C48FT	1990	Ex Wallace Arnold, 1993	National Express
547	G547LWU	Volvo B10M-60	Plaxton Paramount 3500 III	C48FT	1990	Ex Wallace Arnold, 1993	National Express
548	G548LWU	Volvo B10M-60	Plaxton Paramount 3500 III	C48FT	1990	Ex Wallace Arnold, 1993	National Express

CHENERY'S

R.W., P.G. & G. Chenery, The Garage, Dickleburgh, Diss, Norfolk, IP21 4NJ

599 London–Norwich Castle

UPV337	Kässbohrer Setra S215HR	Kässbohrer Rational	C49FT	1987	Ex Bebb, Llantwit Fardre, 1989	Rapide
H62PDW	Kässbohrer Setra S215HD	Kässbohrer Tornado	C49FT	1991	Ex Bebb, Llantwit Fardre, 1993	Rapide
H63PDW	Kässbohrer Setra S215HD	Kässbohrer Tornado	C49FT	1991	Ex Bebb, Llantwit Fardre, 1993	Rapide
H64PDW	Kässbohrer Setra S215HD	Kässbohrer Tornado	C49FT	1991	Ex Bebb, Llantwit Fardre, 1993	Rapide
RYG684	Kässbohrer Setra S215HD	Kässbohrer Tornado	C49FT	1994		Rapide

Previous Registration
UPV337   D704NUH

COSGROVE'S

Cosgroves Hire Services Ltd, 133 Woodplumpton Road, Cadley, Preston, Lancashire, PR2 2LS

646 Burnley–Pwllheli (Saturday Only)

	E331EVH	DAF SB2305DHTD585	Plaxton Paramount 3200 III	C53F	1988		White
	G225HCP	DAF SB3000DKV601	Van Hool Alizée	C51FT	1990		White
	G226HCP	DAF SB3000DKV601	Van Hool Alizée	C51FT	1990		White
	M639RCP	DAF DE33WSB3000	Van Hool Alizée	C51FT	1995		White

CUMBERLAND

Cumberland Motor Services Ltd, PO Box 17, Tangier Street, Whitehaven, Cumbria, CA28 7XF

398 Leicester–Whitehaven
570 London–Blackpool
590 London–Aberdeen
570 London–Barrow
570 London–Whitehaven

120	J120AHH	Volvo B10M-60	Plaxton Expressliner	C46FT	1991		Rapide
121	J121AHH	Volvo B10M-60	Plaxton Expressliner	C46FT	1991		Rapide
125	L125NAO	Volvo B10M-62	Plaxton Expressliner II	C46FT	1994		Rapide
126	L126NAO	Volvo B10M-62	Plaxton Expressliner II	C46FT	1994		Rapide
127	L127NAO	Volvo B10M-62	Plaxton Expressliner II	C46FT	1994		Rapide
128	N128VAO	Volvo B10M-62	Plaxton Expressliner II	C44FT	1995		Rapide
129	N129VAO	Volvo B10M-62	Plaxton Expressliner II	C44FT	1995		Rapide
130	N130VAO	Volvo B10M-62	Plaxton Expressliner II	C44FT	1995		Rapide
131	N131VAO	Volvo B10M-62	Plaxton Expressliner II	C44FT	1995		Rapide
132	N132VAO	Volvo B10M-62	Plaxton Expressliner II	C44FT	1995		Rapide

DORSET TRAVEL

Dorset Travel Services Ltd, Transport Depot, Mallard Road, Bournemouth, Dorset, BH8 9PN

065 London–Portsmouth
072 London–Bournemouth
072 London–Southsea
075 London–Portsmouth
075 London–Southsea

300 Bristol–Southsea
335 Bournemouth–Halifax
333 Blackpool–Bournemouth
515 London–Bournemouth
515 London–Poole

515 London–Poole Ferry
515 London–Weymouth
680 London–Alton Towers

331	L331BFX	MAN 16.290 HOCL	Berkhof Excellence 2000 HL	C49FT	1993			National Express
332	L332BFX	MAN 16.290 HOCL	Berkhof Excellence 2000 HL	C49FT	1993			National Express
336	PJI3354	Volvo B10M-60	Plaxton Paramount 3500 III	C47FT	1991	Ex Park's, 1992		Rapide
337	H371VCG	Volvo B10M-60	Plaxton Paramount 3500 III	C49FT	1991	Ex Park's, 1992		Rapide
338	H338KPR	Volvo B10M-60	Plaxton Expressliner	C46FT	1990			Rapide
339	H339KPR	Volvo B10M-60	Plaxton Expressliner	C46FT	1990			Rapide
340	J40DTS	Volvo B10M-60	Plaxton Expressliner	C49FT	1990			National Express
349	H349MLJ	Volvo B10M-60	Plaxton Expressliner	C46FT	1990			Rapide
350	J50DTS	Volvo B10M-60	Plaxton Expressliner	C46FT	1990			Rapide
351	H351MLJ	Volvo B10M-60	Plaxton Expressliner	C49FT	1990			National Express
352	H352MLJ	Volvo B10M-60	Plaxton Expressliner	C49FT	1990			National Express
353	H353MLJ	Volvo B10M-60	Plaxton Expressliner	C49FT	1990			National Express
354	K354VRU	Volvo B10M-60	Plaxton Expressliner II	C49FT	1991			National Express
355	K355VRU	Volvo B10M-60	Plaxton Expressliner II	C49FT	1991			National Express
356	M356LFX	Scania K113CRB	Van Hool Alizée	C49FT	1995			National Express
357	M357LFX	Scania K113CRB	Van Hool Alizée	C49FT	1995			National Express
358	M358LFX	Scania K113CRB	Van Hool Alizée	C49FT	1995			National Express
359	M359LFX	Scania K113CRB	Van Hool Alizée	C49FT	1995			National Express
360	M360LFX	Scania K113CRB	Van Hool Alizée	C49FT	1995			National Express
361	M361LFX	Scania K113CRB	Van Hool Alizée	C44FT	1995			Rapide
362	M362LFX	Scania K113CRB	Van Hool Alizée	C44FT	1995			Rapide
363	M363LFX	Scania K113CRB	Van Hool Alizée	C44FT	1995			Rapide
364	M364LFX	Scania K113CRB	Van Hool Alizée	C44FT	1995			Rapide
365	M365LFX	Scania K113CRB	Van Hool Alizée	C44FT	1995			Rapide
366	M366LFX	Scania K113CRB	Van Hool Alizée	C44FT	1995			Rapide

Previous Registrations:

PJI3354   H815AHS   H371VCG   H818AHS, PJI3354

DURHAM TRAVEL

Durham Travel Services Ltd, Byron House, Seaham Grange Industrial Estate, Seaham, County Durham, SR7 0PW

065 London–Portsmouth	526 London–Sunderland	563 London–Whitby
394 Glasgow–Newcastle	545 London–Birmingham	591 London–Edinburgh
524 London–Newcastle	561 London–Bradford	663 Newcastle–Fantasy Island
526 London–Hetton-le-Hole	561 London–Keighley	
526 London–South Shields	561 London–Skipton	

1	J1DTS	Aüwaerter Neoplan N122/3	Aüwaerter Skyliner	CH57/22CT	1991		Rapide
2	J2DTS	Aüwaerter Neoplan N122/3	Aüwaerter Skyliner	CH57/22CT	1992		Rapide
3	L3DTS	Scania K113CRB	Van Hool Alizée HE	C42FT	1993		Rapide
4	H4DTS	Aüwaerter Neoplan N122/3	Aüwaerter Skyliner	CH57/22CT	1990		Rapide
5	H5DTS	Aüwaerter Neoplan N122/3	Aüwaerter Skyliner	CH57/22CT	1990		Rapide
22	N22DTS	Volvo B10M-SE	Plaxton Première 350	C44FT	1995		Rapide
23	N23RTN	Volvo B10M-62	Plaxton Expressliner II	C44FT	1996		Rapide
26	J726JFT	Volvo B10M-60	Plaxton Expressliner	C49FT	1991		Rapide
27	J727JFT	Volvo B10M-60	Plaxton Expressliner	C49FT	1991		Rapide
28	L28ABB	Scania K113CRB	Van Hool Alizée HE	C44FT	1994		Rapide
29	L29ABB	Scania K113CRB	Van Hool Alizée HE	C44FT	1994		Rapide
34	M34HJR	Scania K113CRB	Van Hool Alizée HE	C44FT	1995		Rapide
35	H35CNL	Volvo B10M-60	Plaxton Expressliner	C49FT	1990		Rapide
36	M36HJR	Scania K113CRB	Van Hool Alizée HE	C44FT	1995		Rapide
37	M37HJR	Scania K113CRB	Van Hool Alizée HE	C44FT	1995		Rapide
38	M38HJR	Scania K113CRB	Van Hool Alizée HE	C44FT	1995		Rapide
39	M39HJR	Scania K113CRB	Van Hool Alizée HE	C44FT	1995		Rapide
53	H203CRH	Volvo B10M-60	Plaxton Expressliner	C46FT	1991	Ex Kingston-upon-Hull, 1993	Rapide

Previous Registrations:

H4DTS	H881AVK
H5DTS	H882AVK

EAST YORKSHIRE

East Yorkshire Motor Services Ltd, 252 Anlaby Road, Hull, HU3 2RS

322 Scarborough–Swansea	382 Bradford–Liverpool	382 Hull Docks–Liverpool	562 London–Hull
338 Hull–Weymouth	382 Hull–Liverpool	562 London–Beverley	

57	H157AKH	Volvo B10M-60	Plaxton Expressliner	C46FT	1991		Rapide
58	J58ERH	Volvo B10M-60	Plaxton Expressliner	C46FT	1991		Rapide
59	J159HAT	Volvo B10M-60	Plaxton Expressliner	C46FT	1992		Rapide
60	J160HAT	Volvo B10M-60	Plaxton Expressliner	C46FT	1992		Rapide
61	K161TKH	Volvo B10M-60	Plaxton Première 350	C46FT	1993		Rapide
62	L62VAG	Volvo B10M-60	Plaxton Première 350	C46FT	1993		Rapide
64	L64CKH	Volvo B10M-60	Plaxton Première 350	C46FT	1994		Rapide
67	M67LAG	Scania K113CRB	Van Hool Alizée HE	C49FT	1995		National Express
68	M68LAG	Scania K113CRB	Van Hool Alizée HE	C49FT	1995		National Express
70	N170AAG	Scania K113CRB	Van Hool Alizée HE	C49FT	1996		National Express
71	N171AAG	Scania K113CRB	Van Hool Alizée HE	C49FT	1996		National Express
72	N172AAG	Scania K113CRB	Van Hool Alizée HE	C49FT	1996		National Express
73	N173AAG	Scania K113CRB	Van Hool Alizée HE	C49FT	1996		National Express

EMB BUS AND COACH

J R Benson, 2 Redditch Close, Greasby, Wirral, Merseyside, L49 2QJ

647 Rochdale–Pwllheli	732 Liverpool–Perranporth (Weekends)

	G439GJC	Volvo B10M-60	Plaxton Expressliner	C46FT	1990	Ex Selwyns, Runcorn, 1995	White
	H56VRH	Volvo B10M-60	Plaxton Expressliner	C48FT	1990	Ex East Yorkshire, 1996	White

EXCELSIOR

Excelsior Holidays Ltd, 22 Sea Road, Bournemouth, Dorset, BH5 1DD

739 Bournemouth–Edinburgh

801	M801KJT	Volvo B10M-62	Plaxton Expressliner II	C44FT	1994		Rapide
802	M802KJT	Volvo B10M-62	Plaxton Expressliner II	C44FT	1994		Rapide

EXPRESS TRAVEL

Express Travel (Holdings) Ltd, Woodend Avenue, Speke, Liverpool, L24 9NB

074 London–Portsmouth	325 Heathrow–Rochdale	355 Blackpool–Liverpool	383 Edinburgh–Wrexham
303 Southport–Southsea	351 Blackpool–Sheffield	360 Liverpool–Manchester	390 Manchester–Caernarfon
304 Brighton–Liverpool	351 Blackpool–Stockport	380 Leeds–Manchester	390 Manchester–Llandudno

K18AMB	Volvo B10M-60	Plaxton Expressliner II	C46FT	1992		Express Shuttle
K19AMB	Volvo B10M-60	Plaxton Expressliner II	C46FT	1992		Express Shuttle
K20AMB	Volvo B10M-60	Plaxton Expressliner II	C46FT	1992		Express Shuttle
K504WNR	Volvo B10M-60	Plaxton Expressliner II	C46FT	1993		Express Shuttle
K505WNR	Volvo B10M-60	Plaxton Expressliner II	C46FT	1993		Express Shuttle
K506WNR	Volvo B10M-60	Plaxton Expressliner II	C46FT	1993		Rapide
L705PHE	Volvo B10M-62	Van Hool Alizée	C46FT	1994		Rapide
L706PHE	Volvo B10M-62	Van Hool Alizée	C46FT	1994		Rapide
L707PHE	Volvo B10M-62	Van Hool Alizée	C46FT	1994		Rapide
L708PHE	Volvo B10M-62	Van Hool Alizée	C46FT	1994		National Express
L709PHE	Volvo B10M-62	Van Hool Alizée	C46FT	1994		National Express
L710PHE	Volvo B10M-62	Van Hool Alizée	C46FT	1994		National Express
L711PHE	Volvo B10M-62	Van Hool Alizée	C46FT	1994		National Express
L712PHE	Volvo B10M-62	Van Hool Alizée	C46FT	1994		National Express
L713PHE	Volvo B10M-62	Van Hool Alizée	C46FT	1994		National Express
L714PHE	Volvo B10M-62	Van Hool Alizée	C46FT	1994		National Express
M3ERH	Dennis Javelin GX 12SDA2125	Plaxton Expressliner II	C46FT	1995	Ex Roger Hill, Congleton, 1996	Rapide

GALLOWAY

Galloway European Coachlines Ltd, Denters Hill, Mendlesham, Stowmarket, Suffolk, IP14 5RR

011 Bury St Edmunds–London (Sunday)	011 London–Cambridge (Sunday)	081 London–Felixstowe	081 London–Ipswich

5516PP	DAF SB3000DKV601	Van Hool Alizée	C49FT	1992	Ex Amberline, 1994	National Express

Previous Registrations:
5516PP   J811KHD

JONES INTERNATIONAL

M. & M. Jones, Bron-y-de, Gwynfe Road, Ffairfach, Llandeilo, Dyfed, SA19 6UY

321 Birmingham–Swansea   691 Minehead–Swansea

BXI637	Leyland Tiger TRCTL11/3R	Plaxton Paramount 3500	C49FT	1984	Ex Proctor, Fenton, 1988	Yellow with blue relief
B10MMJ	Volvo B10M-61	Van Hool Alizée H	C49FT	1985	Ex Lewis, Whitland, 1993	Yellow with blue relief
730MMJ	DAF MB230LB615	Van Hool Alizée H	C49FT	1987	Ex Welsh, Upton, 1990	Yellow with blue relief

Note: One or two coaches are operated on hire throughout the year when required

Previous Registrations;

730MMJ	E323EVH	B10MMJ	B238VMH, HIL4424	BXI637	DVT994Y

MIDLAND FOX

Midland Fox Ltd, 30 Millstone Lane, Leicester, LE1 5RN

398 Leicester–Manchester   440 London–Leicester
440 London–Burton-on-Trent   440 London–Derby

211	N211TBC	Volvo B10M-62	Plaxton Expressliner II	C49FT	1996		National Express
212	N212TBC	Volvo B10M-62	Plaxton Expressliner II	C49FT	1996		National Express
237	F407DUG	Volvo B10M-60	Plaxton Paramount 3200 III	C50FT	1989	Ex Wallace Arnold, 1992	National Express
246	J246MFP	Volvo B10M-60	Plaxton Paramount 3500 III	C49FT	1992	Ex Express Travel, 1996	National Express
247	J247MFP	Volvo B10M-60	Plaxton Paramount 3500 III	C49FT	1992	Ex Express Travel, 1996	National Express

MOORE COACHES

P.H., D.M. & J.C. Moore, La-Moor, Holmes Chapel Road, Davenport, Congleton, Cheshire, CW12 4SS

521 London–Wrexham	673 Minehead–Stoke (Saturday)	742 Glasgow–Wrexham
609 Manchester–Birmingham (NEC)	738 Manchester Airport–Glasgow (Friday and Sunday)	

112ETU	Hestair Duple SDA1512	Duple 425	C53FT	1987	Ex Abbey Travel, London N10, 1993	Rapide
SJI1972	Van Hool T815	Van Hool Alizée	C49FT	1988	Ex A & R International, Bedfont, 1995	Rapide
G409YAY	Hestair Duple SDA1512	Duple 425	C55F	1990	Ex Bywater, Rochdale, 1994	Rapide
J918LEM	Volvo B10M-60	Plaxton Expressliner	C46FT	1991	Ex Express Travel, 1995	Rapide

Previous Registrations;

112ETU	D525BBV	SJI1972	E276MMM

NORTH DEVON

North Devon Ltd, Coney Avenue, Barnstaple, Devon, EX32 8QJ

339 Cheltenham–Westward Ho!	502 London–Bideford	502 London–Ilfracombe	502 London–Westward Ho!

2228	H228CFJ	Volvo B10M-60	Plaxton Expressliner	C46FT	1991		Rapide
2229	H229CFJ	Volvo B10M-60	Plaxton Expressliner	C46FT	1991		Rapide
2230	920GTA	Volvo B10M-60	Plaxton Expressliner	C49FT	1990	Ex Premier, Cambridge, 1993	National Express
2232	N232WFJ	Dennis Javelin GX 12SDA2153	Plaxton Expressliner II	C44FT	1996		Rapide
2233	N233WFJ	Dennis Javelin GX 12SDA2153	Plaxton Expressliner II	C44FT	1996		Rapide

Previous Registrations;

920GTA	G326PEW

NORTHUMBRIA

Northumbria Motor Services Ltd, 6 Portland Terrace, Jesmond, Newcastle-upon-Tyne, NE2 1QQ

326 Luton Airport–Newcastle
513 London–Bath
525 London–Ashington
525 London–Newcastle

131	K131FKW	Bova FHD12.290	Bova Futura	C44FT	1992		Rapide
132	K132FKW	Bova FHD12.290	Bova Futura	C44FT	1992		Rapide
133	L33NMS	Bova FHD12.340	Bova Futura	C44FT	1993		Rapide
134	NMS700	Bova FHD12.290	Bova Futura	C44FT	1990	Ex Boyden, Castle Donington, 1991	Rapide
135	J20NMS	Bova FHD12.290	Bova Futura	C44FT	1992		Rapide
136	WSV570	Bova FHD12.340	Bova Futura	C44FT	1994		Rapide
137	WSV571	Bova FHD12.340	Bova Futura	C44FT	1994		Rapide
138	WSV572	Bova FHD12.340	Bova Futura	C44FT	1994		Rapide
139	WLT859	Bova FHD12.290	Bova Futura	C46FT	1993		Rapide
140	N122UUB	Bova FHD12.340	Bova Futura	C46FT	1994		Rapide

Previous Registrations:

NMS700	G418WFP	WSV572	L768YTN
WLT859	K121HWF		
WSV570	L766YTN		
WSV571	L767YTN		

PARK'S

Park's of Hamilton (Coach Hirers) Ltd, 41 Bothwell Road, Hamilton, ML3 0AY

737 Glasgow–Lincoln
794 Glasgow–Hull
794 Hull Docks–Glasgow

	M627FNS	Volvo B10M-60	Jonckheere Deauville 45	C47FT	1995	Rapide
	M628FNS	Volvo B10M-60	Jonckheere Deauville 45	C47FT	1995	Rapide
	M629FNS	Volvo B10M-60	Jonckheere Deauville 45	C47FT	1995	Rapide
	M630FNS	Volvo B10M-60	Jonckheere Deauville 45	C47FT	1995	Rapide

PREMIER

Premier Travel Services Ltd, Kilmaine Close, Kings Hedges Road, Cambridge, CB4 2PH

011 London–Cambridge	048 London–Peterborough	305 Cambridge–Liverpool	347 Great Yarmouth–Taunton
048 London–Grimsby	049 London–Mablethorpe	314 Birmingham–Cambridge	350 Cambridge–Liverpool
048 London–Lincoln	303 Birmingham–Liverpool	346 Cambridge–Paignton	350 Liverpool–Sheffield

425	G525LWU	Volvo B10M-60	Plaxton Paramount 3500 III	C49FT	1990	Ex Wallace Arnold, 1994	National Express
426	G526LWU	Volvo B10M-60	Plaxton Paramount 3500 III	C49FT	1990	Ex Wallace Arnold, 1994	National Express
427	G527LWU	Volvo B10M-60	Plaxton Paramount 3500 III	C49FT	1990	Ex Wallace Arnold, 1994	National Express
430	G520LWU	Volvo B10M-60	Plaxton Paramount 3500 III	C49FT	1990	Ex Wallace Arnold, 1994	National Express
431	H649UWR	Volvo B10M-60	Plaxton Paramount 3500 III	C49FT	1991	Ex Wallace Arnold, 1994	National Express
432	H642UWR	Volvo B10M-60	Plaxton Paramount 3500 III	C48FT	1991	Ex Wallace Arnold, 1994	National Express
433	H643UWR	Volvo B10M-60	Plaxton Paramount 3500 III	C48FT	1991	Ex Wallace Arnold, 1994	National Express
434	H652UWR	Volvo B10M-60	Plaxton Paramount 3500 III	C48FT	1991	Ex Wallace Arnold, 1994	National Express
435	H653UWR	Volvo B10M-60	Plaxton Paramount 3500 III	C48FT	1991	Ex Wallace Arnold, 1994	National Express
439	J739CWT	Volvo B10M-60	Plaxton Première 350	C48FT	1992	Ex Wallace Arnold, 1994	National Express
440	J740CWT	Volvo B10M-60	Plaxton Première 350	C48FT	1992	Ex Wallace Arnold, 1994	National Express
441	J741CWT	Volvo B10M-60	Plaxton Première 350	C48FT	1992	Ex Wallace Arnold, 1994	National Express
442	J742CWT	Volvo B10M-60	Plaxton Première 350	C48FT	1992	Ex Wallace Arnold, 1994	National Express
443	J743CWT	Volvo B10M-60	Plaxton Première 350	C48FT	1992	Ex Wallace Arnold, 1994	National Express
444	J744CWT	Volvo B10M-60	Plaxton Première 350	C48FT	1992	Ex Wallace Arnold, 1994	National Express
445	N445XVA	Volvo B10M-62	Plaxton Expressliner II	C49FT	1995		Express Shuttle
446	N446XVA	Volvo B10M-62	Plaxton Expressliner II	C49FT	1995		Express Shuttle
447	N447XVA	Volvo B10M-62	Plaxton Expressliner II	C49FT	1995		Express Shuttle
448	N448XVA	Volvo B10M-62	Plaxton Expressliner II	C49FT	1995		Express Shuttle
449	N449XVA	Volvo B10M-62	Plaxton Expressliner II	C49FT	1995		Express Shuttle
450	N450XVA	Volvo B10M-62	Plaxton Expressliner II	C49FT	1995		Express Shuttle
451	N451XVA	Volvo B10M-62	Plaxton Expressliner II	C49FT	1995		Express Shuttle
452	N452XVA	Volvo B10M-62	Plaxton Expressliner II	C49FT	1995		Express Shuttle

RAPSONS

Rapsons Coaches Ltd, 1 Seafield Road, Longman Industrial Estate, Inverness, IV1 1TN

588 London–Inverness	589 London–Inverness	738 Oxford–Inverness	

ESK986	Volvo B10M-62	Plaxton Première 350	C46FT	1993	Rapide
L592RST	Volvo B10M-62	Plaxton Première 350	C46FT	1993	Rapide
L845RST	Volvo B10M-60	Van Hool Alizée	C44FT	1993	Rapide
N139YST	Volvo B10M-62	Plaxton Expressliner II	C46FT	1995	Rapide
N905AAS	Volvo B10M-62	Plaxton Expressliner II	C46FT	1995	Rapide
N906AAS	Volvo B10M-62	Plaxton Expressliner II	C46FT	1995	Rapide
N764CAS	Volvo B10M-62	Plaxton Première 350	C44FT	1996	Rapide

Previous Registration
ESK986   L591RST

RIBBLE

Ribble Buses, Frenchwood Avenue, Preston, Lancashire, PR1 4LU

480 London–Kidderminster		545 London–Stoke-on-Trent	572 London–Burnley		572 London–Colne	
1122	J122AHH	Volvo B10M-60	Plaxton Expressliner	C46FT	1992	Ex Cumberland, 1995	Rapide
1123	J123AHH	Volvo B10M-60	Plaxton Expressliner	C46FT	1992	Ex Cumberland, 1995	Rapide
1124	J124AHH	Volvo B10M-60	Plaxton Expressliner	C46FT	1992	Ex Cumberland, 1995	Rapide
1164	M164SCK	Volvo B10M-62	Plaxton Expressliner II	C46FT	1994		Rapide
1165	M165SCK	Volvo B10M-62	Plaxton Expressliner II	C46FT	1994		Rapide

RIDER GROUP

Rider Group, Network House, Stubbs Beck Lane, West 26 Ind Est, Cleckheaton, BD19 4TT

310 Southsea–Bradford		380 Leeds–Manchester	380 Manchester–Sunderland		608 Bradford–Birmingham (NEC)	
361 Leeds–Manchester		380 Sunderland–Leeds	381 Newcastle–Leeds		653 Skegness–Bradford	
362 Bradford–Manchester						
1419	8995WY	Volvo B10M-60	Plaxton Paramount 3500 III	C49FT	1990	Ex Park's, 1992	National Express
1420	G76RGG	Volvo B10M-60	Plaxton Paramount 3500 III	C49FT	1990	Ex Park's, 1992	Express Shuttle
1421	H841AHS	Volvo B10M-60	Plaxton Paramount 3500 III	C53F	1991	Ex Park's, 1993	Express Shuttle
1423	L511NYG	Volvo B10M-60	Plaxton Première 350	C49FT	1993		National Express
1424	L541XUT	Volvo B10M-62	Plaxton Première 350	C49FT	1994		Express Shuttle
1425	L542XUT	Volvo B10M-62	Plaxton Première 350	C49FT	1994		National Express
1426	L546XUT	Volvo B10M-62	Plaxton Première 350	C49FT	1994		National Express

Previous Registration
8995WY   G73RGG

SCANCOACHES

Scancoaches Ltd, Unit 2 Radford Estate, Old Oak Lane, Harlesden, London, NW10 6UA

683 London–Fantasy Island

L528XUT	Volvo B10M-60	Jonckheere Deauville 45	C51FT	1993		White and blue
L529XUT	Volvo B10M-60	Jonckheere Deauville 45	C51FT	1993		White and blue
L530XUT	Volvo B10M-60	Jonckheere Deauville 45	C51FT	1993		White and blue

SEA VIEW

Seaview Coaches (Poole) Ltd, 10 Fancy Road, Parkstone, Dorset, BH17 7NZ

310 Poole–Bradford

HIL6457	Leyland Tiger TRCTL11/3RZ	Plaxton Paramount 3500	C49F	1985	Ex Shearings, 1990	Grey, red and blue
HIL8416	Leyland Tiger TRCL10/3RZM	Plaxton Paramount 3500 III	C49F	1989	Ex Roe, Stainforth, 1992	Grey, red and blue
J310REL	Volvo B10M-60	Plaxton Paramount 3500 III	C49FT	1991		National Express

Previous Registrations;
HIL6457 B498UNB   HIL8416 F642GET

SELWYNS

Selwyns Travel Ltd, Cavendish Farm Road, Weston, Runcorn, Cheshire, WA7 4LU

546 London–Birkenhead   550 London–Liverpool   692 Liverpool–Birmingham (NEC)   738 Warrington–Edinburgh
546 London–Hoylake   550 London–Southport

38	M366AMA	Dennis Javelin GX 12SDA2125	Plaxton Expressliner	C46FT	1995		Rapide
60	M6SEL	Dennis Javelin GX 12SDA2131	Plaxton Expressliner II	C46FT	1994		Rapide
61	M7SEL	Dennis Javelin GX 12SDA2131	Plaxton Expressliner II	C46FT	1994		Rapide
62	H112OON	Volvo B10M-60	Plaxton Expressliner	C46FT	1991	Ex Express Travel, 1994	Rapide
63	H113OON	Volvo B10M-60	Plaxton Expressliner	C46FT	1991	Ex Express Travel, 1994	Rapide
64	J910OEY	Volvo B10M-60	Plaxton Expressliner	C46FT	1991	Ex Express Travel, 1994	Rapide
67	M365AMA	Dennis Javelin GX 12SDA2125	Plaxton Expressliner II	C46FT	1995		Rapide
68	M255BDM	Volvo B10M-62	Plaxton Expressliner II	C44FT	1995		Rapide
69	M441BDM	Volvo B10M-62	Plaxton Expressliner II	C44FT	1995		Rapide

SHAW HADWIN

John Shaw & Son (Silverdale) Ltd, Stoneleigh, Silverdale, Lancashire, LA5 0RA
Hadwin's Tours Ltd, Stoneleigh, Silverdale, Lancashire, LA5 0RA

066 London–Eastbourne
541 London–Burnley
570 London–Fleetwood
571 London–Blackpool
645 Skegness–Liverpool
690 Liverpool–Alton Towers
646 Manchester–Pwllheli (Mondays and Fridays Only)

H538SEO	Volvo B10M-60	Plaxton Expressliner	C46FT	1991		Rapide
H539SEO	Volvo B10M-60	Plaxton Expressliner	C46FT	1991		Rapide
K615EEO	Volvo B10M-60	Van Hool Alizée	C46FT	1993		Rapide
N160GRN	Volvo B10M-62	Plaxton Première 350	C48FT	1995		Rapide

DON SMITH'S

D.A. Smith & S.A. Reekie, 4 The Crofts, Murton, Seaham, County Durham, SR7 9PB

662 Middlesbrough–Heads of Ayr

HIL5837	Volvo B10M-61	Caetano Algarve	C49FT	1986	Ex Crawley Luxury, 1993	Cream and green
HIL5834	Volvo B10M-61	Plaxton Paramount 3500 III	C51FT	1988		Cream and green
HIL5835	Volvo B10M-61	Van Hool Alizée	C51FT	1988		Cream and green
L289CJR	Volvo B10M-62	Plaxton Première 350	C49FT	1994		Cream and green
N120RJF	Volvo B10M-62	Jonckheere Deauville 45	C49FT	1996		Cream and green

Previous Registrations;

HIL5834	F247OFP	HIL5835	E273HRY	HIL5837	C622KDS, CLC145, C304CAP

SWT

South Wales Transport Ltd, Heol Gwyrosydd, Penlan, Swansea, SA5 7BN

201 Gatwick–Swansea	508 London–Llanelli	708 Birmingham–Haverfordwest
508 London–Haverfordwest	508 London–Swansea	

102	J2SWT	Volvo B10M-60	Plaxton Expressliner II	C49FT	1992	Rapide
103	J3SWT	Volvo B10M-60	Plaxton Expressliner II	C49FT	1992	Rapide
104	J4SWT	Volvo B10M-60	Plaxton Expressliner II	C49FT	1992	AirLink
105	J5SWT	Volvo B10M-60	Plaxton Expressliner II	C49FT	1992	AirLink
106	L506GEP	Volvo B10M-60	Plaxton Expressliner II	C46FT	1993	AirLink
107	M107NEP	Dennis Javelin GX 12SDA2132	Plaxton Expressliner II	C44FT	1994	AirLink
108	M108NEP	Dennis Javelin GX 12SDA2132	Plaxton Expressliner II	C44FT	1994	AirLink
109	M109PWN	Dennis Javelin GX 12SDA2153	Plaxton Expressliner II	C44FT	1995	AirLink
110	M110PWN	Dennis Javelin GX 12SDA2153	Plaxton Expressliner II	C44FT	1995	AirLink
111	M111PWN	Dennis Javelin GX 12SDA2153	Plaxton Expressliner II	C44FT	1995	AirLink
112	N112EWJ	Dennis Javelin GX 12SDA2153	Plaxton Expressliner II	C44FT	1996	Rapide
113	N113VWN	Dennis Javelin GX 12SDA2153	Plaxton Expressliner II	C44FT	1996	Rapide
114	N114VWN	Dennis Javelin GX 12SDA2153	Plaxton Expressliner II	C44FT	1996	Rapide
115	N115VWN	Dennis Javelin GX 12SDA2153	Plaxton Expressliner II	C44FT	1996	Rapide

SPEEDLINK

Speedlink Airport Services Ltd, 106/7 Ashdown House, Gatwick Airport, West Sussex, RH6 0JH

064 London–Brighton	064 London–Seaford	665 London–Bognor Regis
064 London–Newhaven	066 London–Hastings	

V18	K80SAS	Volvo B10M-60	Plaxton Expressliner II	C49FT	1993	National Express
V40	N40SLK	Volvo B10M-62	Plaxton Expressliner II	C49FT	1996	Express Shuttle
V50	N50SLK	Volvo B10M-62	Plaxton Expressliner II	C49FT	1996	Express Shuttle
V51	G251VPK	Volvo B10M-60	Plaxton Expressliner	C46FT	1990	Rapide
V52	G252VPK	Volvo B10M-60	Plaxton Expressliner	C46FT	1990	Rapide
V53	G253VPK	Volvo B10M-60	Plaxton Expressliner	C46FT	1990	Rapide
V54	G254VPK	Volvo B10M-60	Plaxton Expressliner	C46FT	1990	Rapide
V55	G255VPK	Volvo B10M-60	Plaxton Expressliner	C46FT	1990	Rapide
V60	N60SLK	Volvo B10M-62	Plaxton Expressliner II	C49FT	1996	Express Shuttle
V70	N70SLK	Volvo B10M-62	Plaxton Expressliner II	C49FT	1996	Express Shuttle
V80	N80SLK	Volvo B10M-62	Plaxton Expressliner II	C49FT	1996	Express Shuttle
V90	N90SLK	Volvo B10M-62	Plaxton Expressliner II	C49FT	1996	Express Shuttle

STAGECOACH MIDLAND RED

Midland Red (South) Ltd, Railway Terrace, Rugby, Warwickshire, CV21 3HS

| 310 Bradford–Leicester | 322 Birmingham–York | 325 Bolton–Heathrow | 460 London–Stratford-upon-Avon |
| 320 Birmingham–Bradford | 325 Bolton–Coventry | 460 London–Coventry | |

60	G528LWU	Volvo B10M-60	Plaxton Paramount 3500 III	C48FT	1990	Ex Wallace Arnold, 1993	National Express
61	G529LWU	Volvo B10M-60	Plaxton Paramount 3500 III	C48FT	1990	Ex Wallace Arnold, 1993	National Express
62	G530LWU	Volvo B10M-60	Plaxton Paramount 3500 III	C48FT	1990	Ex Wallace Arnold, 1993	National Express
63	G531LWU	Volvo B10M-60	Plaxton Paramount 3500 III	C48FT	1990	Ex Wallace Arnold, 1993	National Express
64	G532LWU	Volvo B10M-60	Plaxton Paramount 3500 III	C48FT	1990	Ex Wallace Arnold, 1993	National Express
65	G535LWU	Volvo B10M-60	Plaxton Paramount 3500 III	C48FT	1990	Ex Wallace Arnold, 1993	National Express

STAGECOACH SOUTH

Stagecoach (South) Ltd, Lewes Enterprise Centre, 112 Malling Street, Lewes, East Sussex, BN7 2RB

| 001 London–Ramsgate | 007 London–Deal | 007 London–Sandwich | 066 London–Hastings |
| 001 London–Westwood | 007 London–Dover | 008 London–Dover | 067 London–Hastings |

8901	G901PKK	Volvo B10M-60	Plaxton Expressliner	C49FT	1989	Ex East Kent, 1993	National Express
8903	G903PKK	Volvo B10M-60	Plaxton Expressliner	C49FT	1989	Ex East Kent, 1993	National Express
8909	J909NKP	Volvo B10M-60	Plaxton Expressliner	C49FT	1992	Ex East Kent, 1993	National Express
8910	K910TKP	Volvo B10M-60	Plaxton Expressliner II	C49FT	1993	Ex East Kent, 1993	National Express
8911	M911WJK	Volvo B10M-62	Plaxton Expressliner II	C49FT	1994		National Express
8912	M912WJK	Volvo B10M-62	Plaxton Expressliner II	C49FT	1994		National Express
8913	M913WJK	Volvo B10M-62	Plaxton Expressliner II	C49FT	1994		National Express
8914	M914WJK	Volvo B10M-62	Plaxton Expressliner II	C49FT	1994		National Express
8915	M915WJK	Volvo B10M-62	Plaxton Expressliner II	C49FT	1994		National Express
8916	M916WJK	Volvo B10M-62	Plaxton Expressliner II	C49FT	1994		National Express
8917	M917WJK	Volvo B10M-62	Plaxton Expressliner II	C49FT	1994		National Express
8918	M918WJK	Volvo B10M-62	Plaxton Expressliner II	C49FT	1994		National Express

TRATHENS

Trathens Travel Services Ltd, Burrington Way, Plymouth, Devon, PL5 3LS

225 Gatwick–Colne	500 London–Plymouth	540 London–Heywood
323 Plymouth–Bradford	501 London–Brixham	540 London–Manchester
325 London–Burnley	501 London–Paignton	540 London–Rochdale
342 Totnes–Rochdale	501 London–Plymouth	570 London–Blackpool
421 London–Blackpool	501 London–Totnes	592 London–Aberdeen
440 London–Manchester	504 London–Penzance	738 Manchester Airport–Aberdeen

Reg	Chassis	Body	Seating	Year	Notes	
NXI1610	Aüwaerter Neoplan N122/3	Aüwaerter Skyliner	CH53/17CT	1988	Ex Happy Days, Woodseaves, 1991	Rapide
F515ETA	Aüwaerter Neoplan N122/3	Aüwaerter Skyliner	CH53/17CT	1988	Ex YellowayTrathens, 1990	Rapide
MBZ1759	Aüwaerter Neoplan N122/3	Aüwaerter Skyliner	CH57/20CT	1989	Ex Mandale, Greystoke, 1993	Rapide
H981GDV	Aüwaerter Neoplan N122/3	Aüwaerter Skyliner	CH53/17CT	1991		Rapide
H982GDV	Aüwaerter Neoplan N122/3	Aüwaerter Skyliner	CH53/17CT	1991		Rapide
J301FSR	Aüwaerter Neoplan N122/3	Aüwaerter Skyliner	CH53/17CT	1992	Ex Express Travel, 1993	Rapide
J449NTT	Aüwaerter Neoplan N122/3	Aüwaerter Skyliner	CH53/17CT	1992		Rapide
J450NTT	Aüwaerter Neoplan N122/3	Aüwaerter Skyliner	CH53/17CT	1992		Rapide
K302JTS	Aüwaerter Neoplan N122/3	Aüwaerter Skyliner	CH53/17CT	1992		Rapide
K701TTA	Aüwaerter Neoplan N122/3	Aüwaerter Skyliner	CH53/17CT	1992		Rapide
L976KDT	Volvo B12T	Van Hool Astrobel	CH57/14CT	1993		Rapide
L977KDT	Volvo B12T	Van Hool Astrobel	CH57/14CT	1993		Rapide
M863TYC	Volvo B12T	Van Hool Astrobel	CH57/14CT	1994		Rapide
M864TYC	Volvo B12T	Van Hool Astrobel	CH57/14CT	1994		Rapide
M865TYC	Volvo B12T	Van Hool Astrobel	CH57/14CT	1994		Rapide
M422VYD	Volvo B10M-62	Van Hool Alizée	C44FT	1995		Rapide
N311BYA	Volvo B10M-62	Van Hool Alizée	C44FT	1995		Rapide
N312BYA	Volvo B10M-62	Van Hool Alizée	C44FT	1995		Rapide
N313BYA	Volvo B10M-62	Van Hool Alizée	C44FT	1995		Rapide
N314BYA	Volvo B10M-62	Van Hool Alizée	C44FT	1995		Rapide
N315BYA	Volvo B12T	Van Hool Astrobel	CH57/14CT	1995		Rapide
N316BYA	Volvo B12T	Van Hool Astrobel	CH57/14CT	1995		Rapide
N318BYA	Volvo B12T	Van Hool Astrobel	CH57/14CT	1995		Rapide
N319BYA	Volvo B12T	Van Hool Astrobel	CH57/14CT	1995		Rapide
N753CYA	Volvo B10M-62	Van Hool Alizée	C44FT	1996		Rapide
N754CYA	Volvo B12T	Van Hool Astrobel	CH57/14CT	1996		Rapide
N755CYA	Volvo B12T	Van Hool Astrobel	CH57/14CT	1996		Rapide
N708CYC	Volvo B12T	Van Hool Astrobel	CH57/14CT	1996		Rapide

Previous Registrations;

MBZ1759	F626CWJ	NXI1610	E111KFA

TRENT

Trent Motor Traction Company Ltd, 21 Uttoxeter New Road, Derby, DE22 3NL

326 Nottingham–Newcastle
440 London–Derby
440 London–Heanor
450 London–Alfreton
450 London–Mansfield
450 London–Retford
460 London–Coventry
604 Nottingham–Birmingham (NEC)

1	L801MRA	Volvo B10M-60	Plaxton Expressliner II	C49FT	1993		National Express
2	L802MRA	Volvo B10M-60	Plaxton Expressliner II	C49FT	1993		National Express
3	L803MRA	Volvo B10M-60	Plaxton Expressliner II	C49FT	1993		National Express
4	L804MRA	Volvo B10M-60	Plaxton Expressliner II	C49FT	1993		National Express
5	L805MRA	Volvo B10M-60	Plaxton Expressliner II	C49FT	1993		National Express
6	L806MRA	Volvo B10M-60	Plaxton Expressliner II	C49FT	1993		National Express
7	L807MRA	Volvo B10M-60	Plaxton Expressliner II	C49FT	1993		National Express
8	L808MRA	Volvo B10M-60	Plaxton Expressliner II	C49FT	1993		National Express

UNITED COUNTIES

United Counties Omnibus Company Ltd, Rothersthorpe Avenue, Northampton, NN4 9UT

055 Weston Favell–London
055 London–Northampton
055 London–Rugby
347 Bristol–Cambridge
348 Bristol–Corby
676 Northampton–Minehead

92	J430HDS	Volvo B10M-60	Plaxton Première 350	C49FT	1992	Ex Park's, 1993	National Express
93	J439HDS	Volvo B10M-60	Plaxton Première 350	C49FT	1992	Ex Park's, 1993	National Express
94	J445HDS	Volvo B10M-60	Plaxton Première 350	C49FT	1992	Ex Rainworth Travel, 1993	National Express
95	J446HDS	Volvo B10M-60	Plaxton Première 350	C49FT	1992	Ex Rainworth Travel, 1993	National Express
96	J450HDS	Volvo B10M-60	Plaxton Première 350	C49FT	1992	Ex Park's, 1993	National Express

VOYAGER

Northern National Omnibus Company Ltd, 117 Queen Street, Gateshead, Tyne & Wear, NE8 2UA

380 Liverpool–Newcastle	381 Chester–York	710 Newcastle–Plymouth
380 Manchester–Newcastle	480 London–Birmingham	711 Bournemouth–Newcastle
381 Chester–Newcastle	709 Birmingham–Newcastle	780 Manchester Airport–Newcastle

7039	H139CVK	Volvo B10M-60	Plaxton Expressliner	C46FT	1991		Rapide
7040	H140CVK	Volvo B10M-60	Plaxton Expressliner	C46FT	1991		Rapide
7041	H141CVK	Volvo B10M-60	Plaxton Expressliner	C46FT	1991		Rapide
7042	H142CVK	Volvo B10M-60	Plaxton Expressliner	C46FT	1991		Rapide
7043	H329UWT	Volvo B10M-60	Plaxton Expressliner	C46FT	1990	Ex Yorkshire Voyager, 1991	Rapide
7044	H330UWT	Volvo B10M-60	Plaxton Expressliner	C46FT	1990	Ex Yorkshire Voyager, 1991	Rapide
7046	JSK346	Volvo B10M-60	Plaxton Paramount 3500 III	C49FT	1990	Ex Hill's of Tredegar, 1992	Rapide
7052	K2VOY	Volvo B10M-60	Plaxton Paramount 3500 III	C46FT	1993		Rapide
7053	K3VOY	Volvo B10M-60	Plaxton Paramount 3500 III	C49FT	1993		Rapide
7058	M58LBB	Volvo B10M-60	Plaxton Expressliner II	C46FT	1995		Rapide
7059	M59LBB	Volvo B10M-60	Plaxton Expressliner II	C46FT	1995		Rapide
7060	N760RCU	Volvo B10M-62	Plaxton Expressliner II	C46FT	1996		Rapide
7061	N761RCU	Volvo B10M-62	Plaxton Expressliner II	C46FT	1996		Rapide

Previous Registrations:

JSK346	G61RGG

WALTONS

P.J.Walton, 111 Bush Lane, Freckleton, Preston, Lancashire, PR4 1SB

640 Blackpool–Alton Towers	643 Preston–Skegness

CIB347	Hestair Dennis SDAK1504	Duple 425	C54FT	1987	Ex Mairs, Aberdeen, 1992
TIB4568	Bova FHD12.290	Bova Futura	C34FTL	1989	Ex Jumbo Ambulance Project, 1996
K530EHE	Scania K93CRB	Plaxton Paramount 3500 III	C51FT	1992	Ex Swanbrook, Cheltenham, 1995

Previous Registrations:

CIB347	D108XSS, PSU626, D35BRS	KIB289	JAM922W	MIW4852	B468MLN	TIB4568	F940MBB

WESSEX

Wessex National Ltd, Premier House, Sussex Street, St.Phillips, Bristol, BS2 0RB

084 London–Clacton
084 London–Walton-on-the-Naze
200 Bristol–Gatwick
305 Southend–Liverpool
320 Birmingham–Bradford

325 Luton–Birmingham
331 Bristol–Bristol Airport
332 Bristol–Bradford
332 Bristol–Birmingham (Sunday)
337 Brixham–Coventry

339 Gloucester–Birmingham
339 Bristol–Birmingham
400 London–Bristol
511 London–Great Malvern
545 London–Birmingham

595 Gatwick–Glasgow
597 London–Lowestoft
607 Bristol–Birmingham (NEC)
670 Coventry–Alton Towers
674 Birmingham–Pwllheli

140	H68PDW	Volvo B10M-60	Plaxton Paramount 3500 III	C49FT	1991	Ex Bebb, Llantwit Fardre, 1993	National Express
141	H69PDW	Volvo B10M-60	Plaxton Paramount 3500 III	C49FT	1991	Ex Bebb, Llantwit Fardre, 1993	National Express
142	H71PWO	Volvo B10M-60	Plaxton Paramount 3500 III	C49FT	1991	Ex Bebb, Llantwit Fardre, 1993	National Express
144	E944LAE	Iveco Daily 49.10	Robin Hood City Nippy	C17F	1988	Ex City Line, 1991	
145	H201JHP	Peugeot-Talbot	Peugeot-Talbot Pullman	B22F	1990	Ex Midland Red West, 1995	AirLink
154	J429GHT	Volvo B10M-60	Plaxton Expressliner	C46FT	1991		Rapide
155	J430GHT	Volvo B10M-60	Plaxton Expressliner	C46FT	1991		Rapide
156	J431GHT	Volvo B10M-60	Plaxton Expressliner	C46FT	1991		Rapide
157	J203HWS	Volvo B10M-60	Plaxton Expressliner	C46FT	1991		Rapide
158	J204HWS	Volvo B10M-60	Plaxton Expressliner	C46FT	1991		Rapide
159	K509NOU	Volvo B10M-60	Plaxton Expressliner II	C46FT	1993		AirLink
160	K991OEU	Volvo B10M-60	Plaxton Expressliner II	C46FT	1993		National Express
161	K792OTC	Volvo B10M-60	Plaxton Expressliner II	C46FT	1993		AirLink
162	K793OTC	Volvo B10M-60	Plaxton Expressliner II	C46FT	1993		AirLink
163	K794OTC	Volvo B10M-60	Plaxton Expressliner II	C46FT	1993		AirLink
166	L64OUO	Volvo B10M-62	Plaxton Expressliner II	C46FT	1993		AirLink
167	L67OUO	Volvo B10M-62	Plaxton Expressliner II	C49FT	1993		AirLink
169	M92BUO	Volvo B10M-62	Plaxton Expressliner II	C46FT	1994		AirLink
171	H72PWO	Volvo B10M-60	Plaxton Expressliner	C49FT	1991	Ex Express Travel, 1994	National Express
174	M763CWS	Volvo B10M-62	Plaxton Expressliner II	C44FT	1994		AirLink
175	M764CWS	Volvo B10M-62	Plaxton Expressliner II	C44FT	1994		AirLink
176	M765CWS	Volvo B10M-62	Plaxton Expressliner II	C46FT	1994		National Express
177	M413DEV	Volvo B10M-62	Plaxton Expressliner II	C44FT	1995		AirLink
178	M439FHW	Volvo B10M-62	Plaxton Expressliner II	C46FT	1995		National Express
179	M440FHW	Volvo B10M-62	Plaxton Expressliner II	C46FT	1995		National Express
180	M41FTC	Volvo B10M-62	Plaxton Expressliner II	C46FT	1995		AirLink
201	N471KHU	Dennis Javelin GX 12SDA2153	Plaxton Expressliner II	C49FT	1996		National Express
202	N472KHU	Dennis Javelin GX 12SDA2153	Plaxton Expressliner II	C49FT	1996		National Express
203	N473KHU	Dennis Javelin GX 12SDA2153	Plaxton Expressliner II	C49FT	1996		National Express
204	N474KHU	Dennis Javelin GX 12SDA2153	Plaxton Expressliner II	C49FT	1996		National Express
205	N913KHW	Dennis Javelin GX 12SDA2153	Plaxton Expressliner II	C49FT	1996		National Express
206	N914KHW	Dennis Javelin GX 12SDA2153	Plaxton Expressliner II	C49FT	1996		National Express
207	N821KWS	Dennis Javelin GX 12SDA2153	Plaxton Expressliner II	C49FT	1996		National Express
208	N822KWS	Dennis Javelin GX 12SDA2153	Plaxton Expressliner II	C49FT	1996		National Express
209	N319NHY	Dennis Javelin GX 12SDA2153	Plaxton Expressliner II	C49FT	1996		National Express
210	N320NHY	Dennis Javelin GX 12SDA2153	Plaxton Expressliner II	C49FT	1996		National Express
211	N321NHY	Dennis Javelin GX 12SDA2153	Plaxton Expressliner II	C49FT	1996		National Express
212	N322NHY	Dennis Javelin GX 12SDA2153	Plaxton Expressliner II	C49FT	1996		National Express

WESTERN NATIONAL

Western National Ltd, Western House, 38 Lemon Street, Truro, Cornwall, TR1 2NS

315 Brighton–Penzance
330 Penzance–Nottingham
336 Penzance–Edinburgh
340 Paignton–Grimsby
403 London–Bath
404 London–Penzance
504 London–Camborne
505 London–Penzance
686 Plymouth–Minehead
732 Liverpool–Perranporth
736 Newquay–Edinburgh

2101	M101ECV	Volvo B12T	Van Hool Astrobel	CH57/14CT	1995		Rapide
2102	M102ECV	Volvo B12T	Van Hool Astrobel	CH57/14CT	1995		Rapide
2103	M103ECV	Volvo B12T	Van Hool Astrobel	CH57/14CT	1995		Rapide
2243	J243LGL	Volvo B10M-60	Plaxton Expressliner	C46FT	1992		Rapide
2244	J244LGL	Volvo B10M-60	Plaxton Expressliner	C46FT	1992		Rapide
2245	J245LGL	Volvo B10M-60	Plaxton Expressliner	C46FT	1992		Rapide
2246	J246LGL	Volvo B10M-60	Plaxton Expressliner	C46FT	1992		Rapide
2247	F444DUG	Volvo B10M-61	Plaxton Paramount 3500 III	C48FT	1989	Ex Wallace Arnold, 1992	Rapide
2248	F446DUG	Volvo B10M-61	Plaxton Paramount 3500 III	C48FT	1989	Ex Wallace Arnold, 1992	Rapide
2249	K249PCV	Volvo B10M-60	Plaxton Expressliner II	C46FT	1993		Rapide
2250	K250PCV	Volvo B10M-60	Plaxton Expressliner II	C46FT	1993		Rapide
2251	K251PCV	Volvo B10M-60	Plaxton Expressliner II	C46FT	1993		Rapide
2254	L254UCV	Volvo B10M-60	Plaxton Expressliner II	C46FT	1993		Rapide
2255	L255UCV	Volvo B10M-60	Plaxton Expressliner II	C46FT	1993		Rapide
2256	L256UCV	Volvo B10M-60	Plaxton Expressliner II	C46FT	1993		Rapide
2257	L257UCV	Volvo B10M-60	Plaxton Expressliner II	C46FT	1993		Rapide
2258	H613UWR	Volvo B10M-60	Plaxton Paramount 3500 III	C46FT	1991	Ex Wallace Arnold, 1994	Rapide
2259	H614UWR	Volvo B10M-60	Plaxton Paramount 3500 III	C46FT	1991	Ex Wallace Arnold, 1994	Rapide
2260	H615UWR	Volvo B10M-60	Plaxton Paramount 3500 III	C46FT	1991	Ex Wallace Arnold, 1994	Rapide
2301	M301BRL	Volvo B10M-62	Plaxton Expressliner II	C46FT	1994		Rapide
2302	M302BRL	Volvo B10M-62	Plaxton Expressliner II	C46FT	1994		Rapide
2303	M303BRL	Volvo B10M-62	Plaxton Expressliner II	C46FT	1994		Rapide
2402	J703CWT	Volvo B10M-60	Plaxton Première 350	C46FT	1992	Ex Wallace Arnold, 1995	Rapide

WILTS & DORSET

Wilts & Dorset Bus Company Ltd, Towngate House, 2-8 Parkstone Road, Poole, Dorset, BH15 2PR

005 London–Salisbury
005 London–Yeovil

3211	L211CRU	Bova FLD12.270	Bova Futura Club	C49FT	1993	National Express
3212	L212CRU	Bova FLD12.270	Bova Futura Club	C49FT	1993	National Express
3213	L213CRU	Bova FLD12.270	Bova Futura Club	C49FT	1993	National Express

YARDLEY'S

Yardley Travel Ltd, 68 Berkley Road East, Hay Mills, Birmingham, B25 8NP

520 London–Shrewsbury	522 London–Aberystwyth	672 Birmingham–Bognor Regis
520 London–Birmingham	671 Birmingham–Fantasy Island	673 Birmingham–Minehead

	H672OOF	Volvo B10M-60	Plaxton Paramount 3500 III	C51FT	1990	Rapide
	N863WVP	Volvo B10M-62	Plaxton Expressliner II	C44FT	1995	Rapide
	N864WVP	Volvo B10M-62	Plaxton Expressliner II	C44FT	1995	Rapide

YEOMANS

Yeomans Canyon Travel Ltd, 21-23 Three Elms Trading Estate, Hereford, HR4 9PO

503 London–Hereford	512 London–Hereford

55	M341SCJ	Volvo B10M-62	Plaxton Expressliner II	C44FT	1995	Rapide
56	M342SCJ	Volvo B10M-62	Plaxton Expressliner II	C44FT	1995	Rapide
57	M343SCJ	Volvo B10M-62	Plaxton Expressliner II	C44FT	1995	Rapide

YORKSHIRE BUSES

The Yorkshire Woollen District Transport Company Ltd, 24 Barnsley Road, Wakefield, WF1 5JX

240 Gatwick–Bradford

51	M51AWW	Scania K113CRB	Van Hool Alizée HE	C44FT	1995	AirLink
52	M52AWW	Scania K113CRB	Van Hool Alizée HE	C44FT	1995	AirLink
53	M53AWW	Scania K113CRB	Van Hool Alizée HE	C44FT	1995	AirLink
54	M54AWW	Scania K113CRB	Van Hool Alizée HE	C44FT	1995	AirLink
56	M56AWW	Scania K113CRB	Van Hool Alizée HE	C44FT	1995	AirLink

YORKSHIRE TRACTION

The Yorkshire Traction Company Ltd, Upper Sheffield Road, Barnsley, South Yorkshire, S70 4PP

310 Coventry–Bradford	312 Barnsley–Blackpool	351 Blackpool–Sheffield	560 London–Barnsley
310 Poole–Bradford	350 Clacton–Liverpool	351 Blackpool–Manchester	560 London–Rotherham
310 Sheffield–Bradford	350 Liverpool–Sheffield	465 London–Huddersfield	564 London–Halifax

1	6078HE	Scania K93CRB	Plaxton Paramount 3500 III	C46FT	1992		Rapide
2	5562HE	Scania K93CRB	Plaxton Paramount 3500 III	C46FT	1992		Rapide
3	3030HE	Scania K93CRB	Plaxton Paramount 3500 III	C46FT	1992		Rapide
4	6290HE	Scania K93CRB	Van Hool Alizée	C46FT	1992	Ex Barnsley & District, 1995	Rapide
48	PHE692	DAF SB3000DKV601	Van Hool Alizée	C51FT	1989	Ex Barnsley & District, 1995	Rapide
52	NHE340	Volvo B10M-61	Plaxton Paramount 3500 III	C46FT	1988	Ex Shearings, 1992	Rapide
53	L53NWJ	Volvo B10M-60	Plaxton Première 350	C46FT	1993		Rapide
54	L54NWJ	Volvo B10M-60	Plaxton Première 350	C46FT	1993		Rapide
55	M655VWE	Volvo B10M-62	Plaxton Première 350	C46FT	1995		Rapide
56	M656VWE	Volvo B10M-62	Plaxton Première 350	C46FT	1995		Rapide
57	M957VKY	Volvo B10M-62	Plaxton Première 350	C46FT	1995		Rapide
71	2542HE	Scania K93CRB	Plaxton Paramount 3500 III	C46FT	1991		Rapide
75	OHE50	Scania K93CRB	Plaxton Paramount 3500 III	C46FT	1991		Rapide
76	YTC856	Scania K113CRB	Plaxton Paramount 3500 III	C46FT	1990		Rapide
77	2408HE	Scania K113CRB	Plaxton Paramount 3500 III	C46FT	1990		Rapide
78	1619HE	Scania K113CRB	Plaxton Paramount 3500 III	C46FT	1990		Rapide
80	FHE428	Scania K113CRB	Plaxton Paramount 3500 III	C46FT	1990	Ex Shearings, 1993	Rapide
81	N281CAK	Scania K113CRB	Van Hool Alizée	C46FT	1996		Rapide
82	N282CAK	Scania K113CRB	Van Hool Alizée	C46FT	1996		Rapide

Previous Registrations:

1619HE	G78MWJ	5562HE	K802FWE	NHE340	E665UNE
2408HE	G77MWJ	6078HE	K801FWE	OHE50	J964YWJ
2542HE	J293YHE	6290HE	J19ARK	PHE692	F628RJX
3030HE	K803FWE	FHE428	G890VNA	YTC856	G76MWJ

Registration Index

HIL5837	Don Smith	J703CWT	Western National	K660BOH	Birmingham Coach Company
HIL6457	Sea View	J726JFT	Durham Travel	K701TTA	Trathens
HIL8416	Sea View	J727JFT	Durham Travel	K792OTC	Wessex
J1DTS	Durham Travel	J739CWT	Premier	K793OTC	Wessex
J2DTS	Durham Travel	J740CWT	Premier	K794OTC	Wessex
J2SWT	South Wales	J741CWT	Premier	K910TKP	Stagecoach South
J3SWT	South Wales	J742CWT	Premier	K991OEU	Wessex
J4SWT	South Wales	J743CWT	Premier	KIB289	Waltons
J5SWT	South Wales	J744CWT	Premier	KSU462	Armstrong Galley
J20NMS	Northumbria	J909NKP	Stagecoach South	KSU463	Armstrong Galley
J40DTS	Dorset Travel	J910OEY	Selwyns	KSU464	Armstrong Galley
J50DTS	Dorset Travel	J917LEM	Bluebird Buses	L3DTS	Durham Travel
J58ERH	East Yorkshire	J918LEM	Moore's Coaches	L28ABB	Durham Travel
J120AHH	Cumberland	J919LEM	Bluebird Buses	L29ABB	Durham Travel
J121AHH	Cumberland	JSK346	Voyager	L33NMS	Northumbria
J122AHH	Ribble	K2VOY	Voyager	L53NWJ	Yorkshire Traction
J123AHH	Ribble	K3VOY	Voyager	L54NWJ	Yorkshire Traction
J124AHH	Ribble	K18AMB	Express Travel	L62VAG	East Yorkshire
J159HAT	East Yorkshire	K19AMB	Express Travel	L64CKH	East Yorkshire
J160HAT	East Yorkshire	K20AMB	Express Travel	L64OUO	Wessex
J203HWS	Wessex	K80SAS	Speedlink	L67OUO	Wessex
J204HWS	Wessex	K131FKW	Northumbria	L81YBB	Armstrong Galley
J243LGL	Western National	K132FKW	Northumbria	L82YBB	Armstrong Galley
J244LGL	Western National	K161TKH	East Yorkshire	L83YBB	Armstrong Galley
J245LGL	Western National	K249PCV	Western National	L84YBB	Armstrong Galley
J246LGL	Western National	K250PCV	Western National	L125NAO	Cumberland
J246MFP	Midland Fox	K251PCV	Western National	L126NAO	Cumberland
J247MFP	Midland Fox	K302JTS	Trathens	L127NAO	Cumberland
J301FSR	Trathens	K354VRU	Dorset Travel	L211CRU	Wilts & Dorset
J310REL	Sea View	K355VRU	Dorset Travel	L212CRU	Wilts & Dorset
J429GHT	Wessex	K504WNR	Express Travel	L213CRU	Wilts & Dorset
J430GHT	Wessex	K505WNR	Express Travel	L254UCV	Western National
J430HDS	United Counties	K506WNR	Express Travel	L255UCV	Western National
J431GHT	Wessex	K509NOU	Wessex	L256UCV	Western National
J439HDS	United Counties	K524RJX	AJC Coaches	L257UCV	Western National
J445HDS	United Counties	K526RJX	AJC Coaches	L289CJR	Don Smith
J446HDS	United Counties	K530EHE	Waltons	L331BFX	Dorset Travel
J449NTT	Trathens	K531RJX	AJC Coaches	L332BFX	Dorset Travel
J450HDS	United Counties	K615EEO	Shaw Hadwin	L506GEP	South Wales
J450NTT	Trathens	K657BOH	Birmingham Coach Company	L511NYG	Rider Group
J455FSR	Bluebird Buses	K658BOH	Birmingham Coach Company	L528XUT	Scancoaches
J456FSR	Bluebird Buses	K659BOH	Birmingham Coach Company	L529XUT	Scancoaches

Registration	Operator	Registration	Operator	Registration	Operator
L530XUT	Scancoaches	M39KAX	Bebbs	M357LFX	Dorset Travel
L541XUT	Rider Group	M41FTC	Wessex	M358LFX	Dorset Travel
L542XUT	Rider Group	M41KAX	Bebbs	M359LFX	Dorset Travel
L546XUT	Rider Group	M42KAX	Bebbs	M360LFX	Dorset Travel
L592RST	Rapsons	M43KAX	Bebbs	M361LFX	Dorset Travel
L705PHE	Express Travel	M45KAX	Bebbs	M362LFX	Dorset Travel
L706PHE	Express Travel	M51AWW	Yorkshire Buses	M363LFX	Dorset Travel
L707PHE	Express Travel	M52AWW	Yorkshire Buses	M364LFX	Dorset Travel
L708PHE	Express Travel	M53AWW	Yorkshire Buses	M365AMA	Selwyns
L709PHE	Express Travel	M54AWW	Yorkshire Buses	M365LFX	Dorset Travel
L710PHE	Express Travel	M56AWW	Yorkshire Buses	M366AMA	Selwyns
L711PHE	Express Travel	M58LBB	Voyager	M366LFX	Dorset Travel
L712PHE	Express Travel	M59LBB	Voyager	M413DEV	Wessex
L713PHE	Express Travel	M67LAG	East Yorkshire	M422VYD	Trathens
L714PHE	Express Travel	M68LAG	East Yorkshire	M439FHW	Wessex
L801MRA	Trent	M92BOU	Wessex	M440FHW	Wessex
L802MRA	Trent	M101ECV	Western National	M441BDM	Selwyns
L803MRA	Trent	M102ECV	Western National	M627FNS	Park's
L804MRA	Trent	M103ECV	Western National	M628FNS	Park's
L805MRA	Trent	M107NEP	South Wales	M629FNS	Park's
L806MRA	Trent	M108NEP	South Wales	M630FNS	Park's
L807MRA	Trent	M109PWN	South Wales	M639RCP	Cosgroves
L808MRA	Trent	M110PWN	South Wales	M655VWE	Yorkshire Traction
L845RST	Rapsons	M111PWN	South Wales	M656VWE	Yorkshire Traction
L976KDT	Trathens	M164SCK	Ribble	M763CWS	Wessex
L977KDT	Trathens	M165SCK	Ribble	M764CWS	Wessex
M3ERH	Express Travel	M237SOJ	Birmingham Coach Company	M765CWS	Wessex
M6SEL	Selwyns	M255BDM	Selwyns	M784SOF	Birmingham Coach Company
M7SEL	Selwyns	M290FAE	Badgerline	M785SOF	Birmingham Coach Company
M23JDW	Bebbs	M291FAE	Badgerline	M801KJT	Excelsior
M24JDW	Bebbs	M292FAE	Badgerline	M802KJT	Excelsior
M32KAX	Bebbs	M293FAE	Badgerline	M808JTY	Armstrong Galley
M34HJR	Durham Travel	M294FAE	Badgerline	M860TYC	Chalfont Coaches
M34KAX	Bebbs	M295FAE	Badgerline	M861TYC	Chalfont Coaches
M35KAX	Bebbs	M296FAE	Badgerline	M862TYC	Chalfont Coaches
M36HJR	Durham Travel	M301BRL	Western National	M863TYC	Trathens
M36KAX	Bebbs	M302BRL	Western National	M864TYC	Trathens
M37HJR	Durham Travel	M303BRL	Western National	M865TYC	Trathens
M37KAX	Bebbs	M341SCJ	Yeomans	M911WJK	Stagecoach South
M38HJR	Durham Travel	M342SCJ	Yeomans	M912WJK	Stagecoach South
M38KAX	Bebbs	M343SCJ	Yeomans	M913WJK	Stagecoach South
M39HJR	Durham Travel	M356LFX	Dorset Travel	M914WJK	Stagecoach South

M915WJK	Stagecoach South	N212TBC	Midland Fox	N822KWS	Wessex
M916WJK	Stagecoach South	N232WFJ	North Devon	N863WVP	Yardley's
M917WJK	Stagecoach South	N233WFJ	North Devon	N864WVP	Yardley's
M918WJK	Stagecoach South	N281CAK	Yorkshire Traction	N905AAS	Rapsons
M957VKY	Yorkshire Traction	N282CAK	Yorkshire Traction	N906AAS	Rapsons
MBZ1759	Trathens	N311BYA	Trathens	N913KHW	Wessex
MIW4852	Waltons	N312BYA	Trathens	N914KHW	Wessex
N22DTS	Durham Travel	N313BYA	Trathens	NHE340	Yorkshire Traction
N23RTN	Durham Travel	N314BYA	Trathens	NMS700	Northumbria
N40SLK	Speedlink	N315BYA	Trathens	NXI1610	Trathens
N50SLK	Speedlink	N316BYA	Trathens	OHE50	Yorkshire Traction
N60SLK	Speedlink	N318BYA	Trathens	PHE692	Yorkshire Traction
N70SLK	Speedlink	N319BYA	Trathens	PJI3354	Dorset Travel
N80SLK	Speedlink	N319NHY	Wessex	RYG684	Chenery's
N90SLK	Speedlink	N320NHY	Wessex	SJI1972	Moore's Coaches
N46MDW	Bebbs	N321NHY	Wessex	TIB4568	Waltons
N47MDW	Bebbs	N322NHY	Wessex	UPV337	Chenery's
N48MDW	Bebbs	N445XVA	Premier	WLT859	Northumbria
N49MDW	Bebbs	N446XVA	Premier	WSV570	Northumbria
N51MDW	Bebbs	N447XVA	Premier	WSV571	Northumbria
N52MDW	Bebbs	N448XVA	Premier	WSV572	Northumbria
N53MDW	Bebbs	N449XVA	Premier	YTC856	Yorkshire Traction
N112EWJ	South Wales	N450XVA	Premier		
N113EWJ	South Wales	N451XVA	Premier		
N114EWJ	South Wales	N452XVA	Premier		
N115EWJ	South Wales	N471KHU	Wessex		
N120RJF	Don Smith	N472KHU	Wessex		
N122UUB	Northumbria	N473KHU	Wessex		
N128VAO	Cumberland	N474KHU	Wessex		
N129VAO	Cumberland	N618UUS	Bluebird Buses		
N130VAO	Cumberland	N619UUS	Bluebird Buses		
N131VAO	Cumberland	N620UUS	Bluebird Buses		
N132VAO	Cumberland	N683AHL	Birmingham Coach Company		
N139YST	Rapsons	N684AHL	Birmingham Coach Company		
N160GRN	Shaw Hadwin	N708CYC	Trathens		
N170AAG	East Yorkshire	N753CYA	Trathens		
N171AAG	East Yorkshire	N754CYA	Trathens		
N172AAG	East Yorkshire	N755CYA	Trathens		
N173AAG	East Yorkshire	N760RCU	Voyager		
N197DYB	Chalfont Coaches	N761RCU	Voyager		
N198DYB	Chalfont Coaches	N764CAS	Rapsons		
N211TBC	Midland Fox	N821KWS	Wessex		

Routes

001 Stagecoach South
005 Wilts & Dorset
007 Stagecoach South
008 Stagecoach South
011 Premier; Galloway (one rounder Sundays only)
048 Premier
049 Premier
055 United Counties
064 Speedlink
065 Dorset Travel; Durham Travel
066 Stagecoach South.
066 Speedlink (one rounder Sundays only). Shaw Hadwin (one rounder only London - Eastbourne)
067 Stagecoach South
072 Dorset Travel
074 Express Travel
075 Dorset Travel
081 Ambassador; Galloway
084 Wessex
200 Wessex
201 SWT; Bebbs (one rounder).
225 Birmingham Coach Company; Trathens (one rounder).
230 Armstrong Galley
240 Yorkshire Buses
300 Dorset Travel
301 Bebbs
303 Express Travel; Premier
304 Express Travel
305 Premier; Wessex
308 Ambassador
310 (Southsea-Bradford) Rider Group
310 (Birmingham-Bradford) Bebbs
310 (Sheffield-Bradford) Yorkshire Traction
310 (Leicester-Bradford) Stagecoach Midland Red

310 (Coventry-Bradford) Yorkshire Traction
310 (Poole-Bradford) Yorkshire Traction; Sea View (alternate days)
312 Yorkshire Traction
314 Premier
315 Western National
320 (Bradford-Cardiff) Bebbs
320 (Birmingham-Bradford) Bebbs; Stagecoach Midland Red; Wessex
320 (Skipton-Brecon) Bebbs
321 Jones International
322 (Birmingham-York) Stagecoach Midland Red
322 (Scarborough-Swansea) East Yorkshire
323 Trathens
325 (Coventry-Bolton) Stagecoach Midland Red
325 (Bolton-Heathrow) Stagecoach Midland Red
325 (Birmingham-Luton) Wessex (Fridays and Sundays only)
325 (Heathrow-Rochdale) Express Travel
325 (London-Burnley) Trathens
326 (Newcastle-Nottingham) Trent
326 (Luton Airport-Newcastle) Northumbria
330 Western National
331 Wessex
332 Wessex
333 Dorset Travel
335 Dorset Travel
336 Western National
337 Wessex
338 East Yorkshire

339 (Westward Ho! -Cheltenham) North Devon
339 (Birmingham-Gloucester) Wessex
339 (Bristol-Birmingham) Wessex
340 Western National
342 Trathens
346 Premier
347 (Cambridge-Bristol) United Counties
347 (Taunton-Great Yarmouth) Premier
348 United Counties
350 (Clacton-Liverpool) Yorkshire Traction
350 (Cambridge-Liverpool) Premier
350 (Sheffield-Liverpool) Premier; Yorkshire Traction
351 (Blackpool-Sheffield) Express Travel; Yorkshire Traction
351 (Blackpool-Manchester) Yorkshire Traction
351 (Blackpool-Stockport) Express Travel
355 Express Travel
360 Express Travel
361 Rider Group
362 Rider Group
380 (Liverpool-Newcastle) Voyager
380 (Leeds-Manchester) Express Travel; Rider Group (Friday and Sunday only)
380 (Sunderland-Leeds) Rider Group (Friday and Sunday only)
380 (Manchester-Sunderland) Rider Group (Friday and Sunday only)
380 (Manchester-Newcastle) Voyager (Friday and Sunday only)
381 (Chester-Newcastle) Voyager

381 (Newcastle-Leeds) Rider Group (Friday and Sunday only)
382 East Yorkshire
383 Express Travel
387 Birmingham Coach Company
390 (Manchester-Caernarfon) Express Travel
390 (Llandudno-Manchester) Express Travel
394 Durham Travel
398 Cumberland
398 (Manchester-Leicester) Midland Fox (Friday and Sunday only)
400 Wessex
402 Badgerline
403 Badgerline; Western National
404 Western National
412 Cheltenham District
421 Trathens
440 (London-Burton-on-Trent) Midland Fox
440 (London-Buxton) Midland Fox
440 (London-Derby) Midland Fox; Trent
440 (London-Heanor) Trent
440 (London-Leicester) Midland Fox
440 (London-Manchester) Trathens
450 Trent
460 (London-Coventry) Stagecoach Midland Red; Trent
460 (London-Stratford-upon-Avon) Stagecoach Midland Red
465 Yorkshire Traction
480 (London-Birmingham) Voyager
480 (London-Kidderminster) Ribble
495 Ambassador
496 Ambassador
497 Ambassador
500 (London-Plymouth) Trathens

500 (London-Penzance) Western National
501 Trathens
502 North Devon
503 Yeomans
504 (London-Camborne) Western National
504 (London-Penzance) Trathens
505 Western National
508 SWT
509 Bebbs
511 Wessex
512 Yeomans
513 Northumbria
515 Dorset Travel
520 (London-Shrewsbury) Yardley's
520 (London-Wolverhampton) Birmingham Coach Company
521 Moore's
522 Yardley's
524 Durham Travel
525 Northumbria
526 Durham Travel
540 Trathens
541 Shaw Hadwin
545 (London-Stoke-on-Trent) Ribble
545 (London-Holyhead) Birmingham Coach Company
545 (London-Birmingham) Bebbs. Wessex (Friday and Sunday only)
545 (London-Pwllheli) Bebbs

545 (Birmingham-London) Durham Travel
546 Selwyns
550 (London-Liverpool) Bebbs; Selwyns
550 (London-Southport) Selwyns
560 Yorkshire Traction
561 (London-Bradford) AJC Coaches; Durham Travel
561 (London-Keighley) Durham Travel
561 (London-Knaresborough) AJC Coaches
561 (London-Skipton) AJC Coaches; Durham Travel
562 East Yorkshire
563 Durham Travel
564 Yorkshire Travel
570 (London-Barrow) Cumberland
570 (London-Blackpool) Cumberland; Trathens
570 (London-Fleetwood) Shaw Hadwin
570 (London-Whitehaven) Cumberland
571 Shaw Hadwin
572 Ribble
588 Rapson's
589 Rapson's
590 Cumberland
591 Durham Travel
592 Trathens
593 Bluebird Buses
595 Wessex

596 Bluebird Buses
597 Ambassador; Wessex
599 Chenery's
604 Trent
605 Chalfont
607 Wessex
608 Rider Group
609 Moore's
610 Chalfont
640 Waltons
643 Waltons
645 Shaw Hadwin
646 (Burnley-Pwllheli [Sat only]) Cosgrove's
646 (Manchester-Pwllheli [Mon & Fri only]) Shaw Hadwin
647 EMS
650 AJC Coaches
653 Rider Group
657 AJC Coaches
662 Smith's
663 Durham Travel
664 AJC Coaches
665 Speedlink
670 Wessex
671 Yardley's
672 Yardley's
673 (Minehead-Birmingham) Yardley's
673 (Minehead-Stoke) Moore's
674 Wessex
676 United Counties

680 Dorset Travel
683 Scancoaches
685 Chalfont
686 Western National
690 Shaw Hadwin
691 Jones International
692 Selwyns
694 Chalfont
708 SWT
709 Voyager
710 Voyager
711 Voyager
732 Western National; EMS (Weekends Only).
736 Western National
737 Park's
738 (Aberdeen-Manchester Airport) Trathens
738 (Manchester Airport-Glasgow) Moore's
738 (Oxford-Inverness) Rapsons
738 (Warrington-Edinburgh) Selwyns
739 Excelsior
742 Moore's
749 Bebbs
752 Bluebird Buses
780 Voyager
794 Park's

All routes are allocated for standard National Express liveried vehicles except:

Air Link services with dedicated liveried single deckers: 200, 201, 230, 240, 331 (minicoach).
Express Shuttle with single deckers: 011, 064, 360, 361, 362.
London Express: 520.
Rapide services with single deckers: 225, 502, 503, 505, 508, 509, 511, 512, 513, 515, 520 (London-Shrewsbury), 521, 522, 524, 525, 526 (some journeys), 541, 545 (some journeys), 546, 550, 560, 561, 562, 563, 564, 570 (most journeys), 571, 572, 588, 589, 590, 591, 593, 595, 596, 597, 599, 708, 709, 710, 711, 732, 736, 737, 738 (most journeys), 739, 742, 749, 752, 780, 794.
Rapide services with double deckers: 325 (London-Burnley only), 404, 421, 500 (London-Plymouth only), 501, 504, 520 (London-Wolverhampton), 526 (some journeys), 540, 545 (some journeys), 570 (some journeys), 592, 738 (Aberdeen-Manchester Airport only).